The Republican Party
Its Heritage and History

By Fred Schwengel

President, The Republican Heritage Foundation

ACROPOLIS BOOKS LTD.

WASHINGTON, D.C.

The Republican Heritage Seal symbolizes the heritage, history, and challenge of the Republican Party. The immortal words of Abraham Lincoln encircle the seal, reminding us of the party's idealism and challenging us to conserve, strengthen, and protect our daring experiment in self-government. The party's first chief of state, bearing the marks of the terrible struggle to preserve the Union, gazes with hope to the future. Also represented are those institutions that undergird our American system: the family, free enterprise, freedom of worship, and education. The school and the church remind us that intelligence and morality were the virtues on which our nation and the Republican Party were built, and on which they must depend for their continued existence. The symbol of industry reminds us of the abundant life that comes from the free enterprise system. The people pictured represent Americans of all races, creeds, and origins who have made our nation great. The emblems of peace—the dove and olive branch—symbolize the goal of the Republican Party for all humanity. Woven into the seal is the American eagle, representing the patriotism, the freedom, and the pride in America that the Republican Heritage Foundation seeks to encourage.

Contents

FOREWORD BY GERALD R. FORD   5

AUTHOR'S INTRODUCTION   6

PORTRAITS OF GREATNESS:
THE REPUBLICAN HERITAGE GALLERY   7

130 YEARS OF ACHIEVEMENT:
THE STORY OF THE REPUBLICAN PARTY   59

MY 60 YEARS AS A REPUBLICAN:
SOME OBSERVATIONS AND CONCLUSIONS   145

DAY BY DAY
THROUGH THE HISTORY OF THE PARTY   150

AMONG THOSE WORTHY OF NOTE   160

INDEX   163

BIBLIOGRAPHY   165

NOTES ON THE AUTHOR AND THE ILLUSTRATOR   167

Published by Acropolis Books Ltd.
2400 17th Street, N.W., Washington, D.C. 20009

Library of Congress CIP Data on page 166.
ISBN 0-87491-882-0 (hardcover)
0-87491-883-9 (paperback)

Second Edition

*The author wishes to thank Ralph Becker and the Smithsonian Institution's Museum
of American History for the opportunity to photograph the Republican campaign
memorabilia reproduced on the front cover and on pages 7 and 59.*

Gallery Portraits

A Party Is Born   8

The Emancipation Proclamation   10

The Gettysburg Address   12

Lincoln's Second Inaugural   14

The Homestead Act and James Wilson   16

Theodore Roosevelt on America's Natural Resources   18

Gifford Pinchot and Conservation   20

Frederick Seaton and Mission 66   22

The Morrill Land-Grant Act   24

Lewis L. Strauss and Atomic Energy   26

Eisenhower and the Peaceful Use of the Atom   28

The Transcontinental Railroad   30

John Hay and the Panama Canal   32

George Dondero and the St. Lawrence Seaway   34

The Interstate Highway System   36

Free Enterprise—the Fifth Great Freedom   38

The Republican Commitment to Labor   40

Theodore Roosevelt and the Nobel Peace Prize   42

Taft and the Pan-American Union   44

Nicholas Murray Butler and World Peace   46

The Campaign and the Two-Party System   48

The Party's Dedication to Law and Order   50

Herbert Hoover and the Hoover Commission   52

Republican Women Legislators Past and Present   54

Republican Presidents Speak   56

Foreword

A political party should be aware of its heritage—not just the familiar tributes to the party's founders, but also the rich diversity of opinion and even the occasionally sharp debates that truly make the party what it is. One of the special merits of this book is that it sets this worthy objective as one of its goals. *The Republican Party: Its Heritage and History* faithfully chronicles an institution whose openness to the world of contrasting political ideas is a matter of record.

The Republican Party has been a party of the people from its inception, as this volume makes clear. The great tragedy of slavery and the national challenge of westward expansion were the twin forces behind the creation of the Grand Old Party. Out of these issues sprang the party's commitment to freedom and free enterprise, embodied by that wisest of all Republican leaders, Abraham Lincoln.

The Republican Party, to its everlasting credit, led in enacting constitutional guarantees of liberty and voting rights, though the reality often fell far short of such noble standards. From the idealism of Reconstruction, the party seemingly descended into the materialism of the Gilded Age. Propelled kicking and screaming into the 20th century by the remarkable Theodore Roosevelt, the party once again took an active, progressive stance.

Reading the sections on the party's history in the 20th century, I am again forcefully reminded of the cyclical nature of American politics. The progressivism of Theodore Roosevelt was invariably followed by the conservatism of Harding and Coolidge, which in turn was followed by the more active Hoover—a man that I have always believed has not received his proper place in history. As we consider the resurgence of Republicanism after the tragedy of Watergate, we must ponder anew the proper stance of the Republican Party.

In reading this book, one is struck not only by events perhaps long forgotten but also by the power of Republican ideas and personalities. Too often in public life, one tends to assume that our current definitions of political ideas are eternal. History shows they are not. The future of American Republicanism is open to the new approaches of youth, and this book can be a source of inspiration for the next generation of Republican leaders.

A moving feature of this book is the Republican Heritage Gallery, with its colorful artwork and informative vignettes of events and personalities in the Republican past. I am intrigued by the rich symbolism of the Republican Heritage Seal and by the brief reminders of the party's accomplishments given in the day-by-day calendar at the end of the book. Finally, I am impressed by the lessons recounted and the policies set forth in the concluding section, "My 60 Years As A Republican," in which former Congressman Schwengel outlines a policy of moderation that today's Republican leaders would be well advised to consider.

Our party has a proud heritage, and it is our duty to pass it on. Throughout my years of friendship with Fred Schwengel, one aspect of his public life has stood out: He believes we can learn from our past. His book is dedicated to perpetuating the Republican legacy. How well it succeeds will depend on you the reader.

Gerald R. Ford
38th President of the United States

Introduction

What is the heritage of a political party? How does one assess a party that has been in existence for some 130 years? Surely a party must be judged by its accomplishments. If so, the Republican Party long ago qualified for greatness. The party that, among other things, led in saving the Union and abolishing slavery, passed the Homestead Act and Land-Grant College Act, built the Panama Canal, and developed the Interstate Highway System has much of which to be proud.

Perhaps a party is to be measured by its leaders. Once again the Republican Party need not take second place to any political organization. With leaders of the stature of Abraham Lincoln, Theodore Roosevelt, Herbert Hoover, and Dwight D. Eisenhower, to name but a few, the Republican Party has greatly enriched our nation's history.

Perhaps a party is to be gauged by its contributions to American democracy. The Republican Party can take pride in the part it has long played in our two-party system, a system that gives all Americans the opportunity to voice their opinions, needs, and wishes.

Undoubtedly, a party's heritage is all these things: great accomplishments, great leaders, and an abiding dedication to participatory democracy. The features that follow provide a glimpse at some of the many proud moments in the Republican heritage. First, the Republican Heritage Gallery, with its 26 beautiful prints by noted artist Charles McVicker, examines a few of the significant contributions of the party to American life. The following section of the book gives a more in-depth look at the party's history. "My 60 Years As A Republican" summarizes my own experiences as a member of the party. Supplementing the main sections is the segment "Day by Day Through the History of the Party," which provides a partial listing of Republican-related accomplishments for each day of the year. "Among Those Worthy of Note" lists some of the important Republicans of the past and present.

As you will see in these pages, the Republican heritage is the result of the work of millions of Americans living and dead. During my 16 years in Congress as a representative of the state of Iowa, and throughout 20 years as President of the Republican Heritage Foundation, I have become more convinced than ever that the Republican Party truly represents all Americans. In addition to their role in abolishing slavery and passing constitutional amendments to ensure the rights of minorities, Republicans have long been sensitive to the valuable role of women in politics. In 1876, the Republican convention was the first to be addressed by a woman speaker; in 1900, the party was the first to admit women delegates; in the 1920s, it was the first to name women to its executive and national committees; and in 1974, it was the first to name a woman, Mary Louise Smith, as national chairman.

In writing this book, I have tried to produce a party history that is not anti-Democrat but rather pro-Republican, an account that stresses the strengths and virtues of our party. Looking back over the long history of the Republican Party, one sees a heritage that is indeed rich and varied, one far more diverse and open to differing opinions than some dogmatic ideologues would have us believe. It is for the present and future generations to carry on this worthy tradition. To that purpose this book is dedicated.

Fred Schwengel

Fred Schwengel
President, Republican Heritage Foundation

1
Portraits of Greatness
The Republican Heritage Gallery

A selection of the party's notable
contributions to American life, depicted in 26 color
paintings by artist Charles McVicker.

Birth and Founding Principles

In 1854 there appeared in America a new political party, labeled "Republican," with a deep dedication to the principles of the Founding Fathers. Born in the hearts of a people seeking to meet the needs of a nation on the brink of civil war, this party believed in the dream of a greater United States, stretching from the Atlantic to the Pacific, and all of it *free*.

The locations at which these Americans met to make their dream a reality are full of symbolism. They met in a church at Crawfordsville, Iowa, because a moral problem was at stake. They met in a schoolhouse in Ripon, Wisconsin, because education for all the people was at the core of their belief. They met under the open sky in Jackson, Michigan, in 1856, to write their national platform, because only this boundless setting was appropriate to the magnitude of the issues involved.

United under the name Republicans, with Abraham Lincoln as President, they changed the direction of America. In a few short years following the party's foundation, slavery was abolished, the Union was saved, the oceans were joined by a transcontinental railroad, and the United States became strong and secure.

In its more than 130 years of existence, the Grand Old Party has always held to liberalism in issues involving people and conservatism in matters of spending. Writer Helen Virden described the Republican Party as the party "most closely in league with the future . . . a political institution that is long on principle." Dwight D. Eisenhower perfectly captured its spirit when he observed: "It is young—it is confident—it is free."

At the White House on January 1, 1863, the great gnarled hand that "swung the ax in Illinois" paused over a document on the President's desk. Exhausted from shaking hands for three hours during the annual diplomatic reception at the White House, the President feared his trembling hand might be reflected in his signature, and that later generations might think he hesitated. But there was no doubt about the President's resolve. He told the members of his Cabinet grouped around the desk, "I never in my life felt more certain that I was doing right than I do in signing this paper."

Slowly, carefully, and surely, at the bottom of the engrossed document he wrote his signature, "Abraham Lincoln." With that signature the Emancipation Proclamation became official. The proclamation declared that "persons held as slaves" in those areas still in rebellion against the United States "are, and henceforward shall be, free." It did not immediately free any slaves, since those areas still in rebellion were under the military control of the Confederacy. But it did set the moral tone for the remainder of the war, and it led inexorably to the total abolition of slavery by the 13th Amendment, ratified in 1865.

The abolition of slavery, which removed the chains of bondage from more than three million human beings, was the fulfillment of the promise of liberty made by the Founding Fathers and enunciated by Abraham Lincoln. Under Republican leadership, America embraced the objectives of our early patriots, and history proved once again that as we share our freedoms, we all benefit.

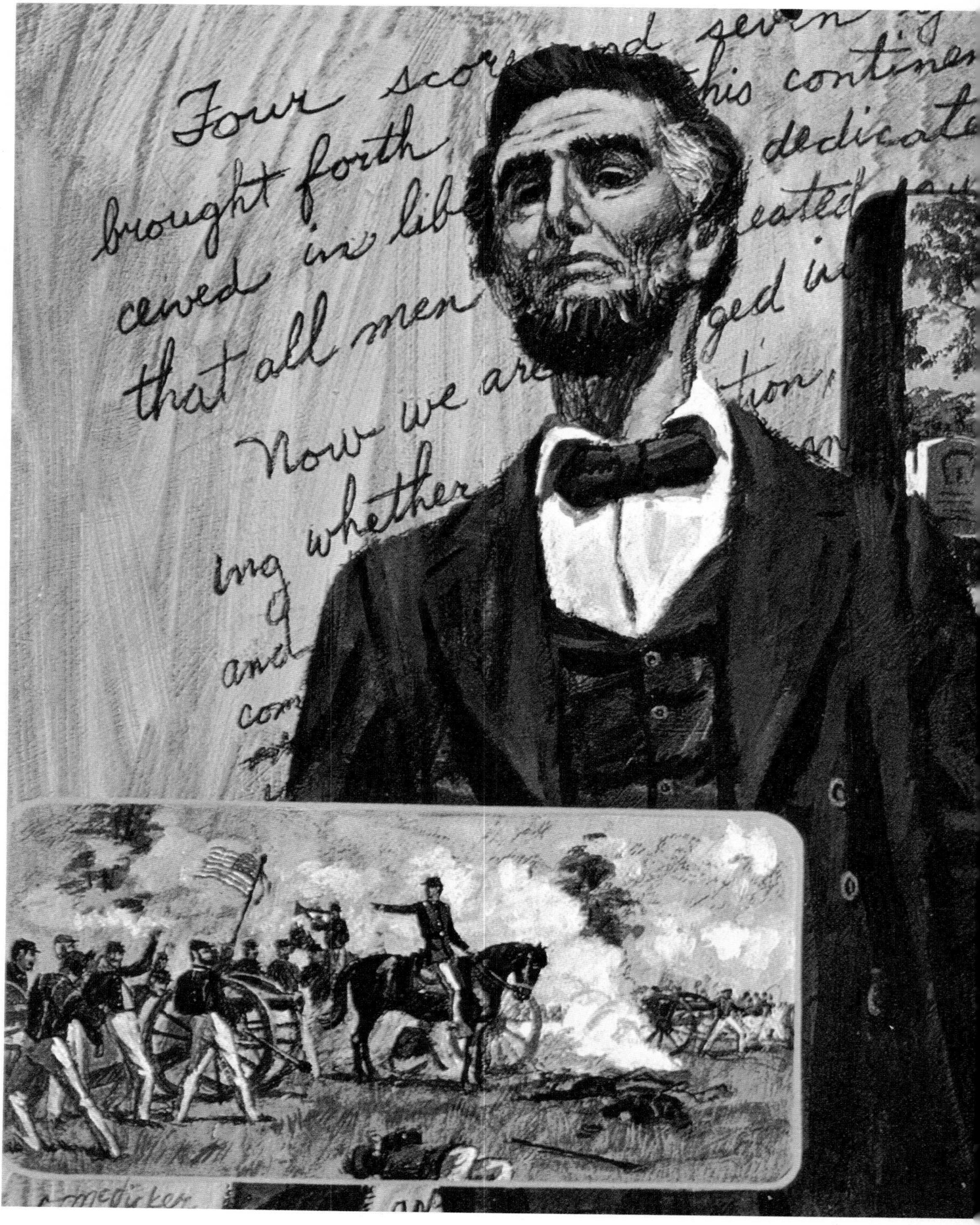
Four
brought forth
dedicate
that all men
Now we are
whether

The Gettysburg Address

The crowd of more than 15,000 spectators was tired and numb from standing throughout Edward Everett's two-hour oration. After a short pause, President Lincoln rose, delivered his brief remarks from a single folded page, and then sat down. The speech was over so quickly that the members of the audience were unaware of the significance of the words they had just heard. They applauded politely, but without enthusiasm. At the time, it might have seemed as if Lincoln had been correct when he said "the world will little note, nor long remember what we say here."

But the world has remembered and will never forget what Abraham Lincoln said at Gettysburg, Pennsylvania, on November 19, 1863, at the dedication of the national cemetery there. The speech had been written in Washington, and Lincoln made minor changes in Gettysburg. In ten sentences and only 268 words, he created a national treasure and a literary masterpiece. Unquestionably the most famous American speech, the Gettysburg Address mirrored the soul of its author and revealed what the Civil War was all about.

The speech, like Lincoln himself, long ago passed beyond the need for praise; it remains now to be appreciated for its beauty and studied for its substance. In its concise sentences are revealed the founding principles of the Republican Party and the promise and challenges of our American democracy. We too must ever resolve "that this nation, under God, shall have a new birth of freedom— and that government of the people, by the people, for the people, shall not perish from the earth."

For four years Lincoln had successfully lead, coaxed, cajoled, and prayed his nation through a terrible struggle, with "sacrifices beyond words to tell" as Carl Sandburg would describe it. The toils and cares of a protracted war were visible in the lines of his noble, craggy face as Lincoln delivered his second inaugural address on March 4, 1865. As Vice President Andrew Johnson, Chief Justice Salmon Chase, and thousands of citizens watched, Lincoln called not for vengeance and retribution, but for healing and reconciliation.

With a military victory close at hand in 1865, there were many in the North, indeed many in the President's own Republican Party, who sought vengeance on the South for the horrible ravages of the Civil War. Lincoln, however, spoke with a wisdom that transcended normal human cares and emotions—a wisdom that still seems sublime, even spiritual. With no rancor or bitterness in his heart, he concluded with a plea—a prayer—for charity and reconciliation:

"With malice toward none, with charity for all; with firmness in the right, as God gives us to see the right, let us strive on to finish the work we are in; to bind up the nation's wounds; to care for him who shall have borne the battle, and for his widow, and his orphan—to do all which may achieve and cherish a just and lasting peace, among ourselves, and with all nations."

Though Lincoln's address was more condemned than commended in 1865, it is recognized today as one of the most eloquent speeches of all time. In his poem, "Lincoln, the Man," Edwin Markham summarized Lincoln's achievement: "When the judgment thunders split the house, wrenching the rafters from their ancient rest, he held the ridgepole up and spiked again the rafters of the home."

Contributions to
Agriculture and Conservation

The Republican Party's contributions to American agriculture have been of immeasurable importance. One of the forces leading to the party's formation was the demand for homestead legislation. The Free Soil Party of the 1840s and 1850s, one of the political factions from which the Republican Party grew, asserted that all men had a natural right to the soil and that the government should grant public lands to landless settlers free of cost.

Objections from southern congressmen kept homestead legislation from passing until 1862, when a Republican-controlled Congress passed the Homestead Act and President Lincoln signed it into law. Under the provisions of the law, any citizen over 21 who was the head of a household could receive a quarter section of land (160 acres) free, provided he lived on and cultivated the land for five years. More than 1,622,000 homesteads were settled, bringing over 270,000,000 acres of land under cultivation. The Homestead Act thereby not only helped settle the West, it also turned the United States into the breadbasket of the world.

James Wilson, nicknamed "Tama Jim" to distinguish him from James F. Wilson, Iowa's other great congressional leader of the period, served in the Cabinet longer than any other man. Secretary of Agriculture from 1897 to 1913, he served under three Republican Presidents: William McKinley, Theodore Roosevelt, and William Howard Taft. His efforts in promoting agricultural experimentation and education resulted in the greatest variety and volume of agricultural research in history. Republican contributions through the Homestead Act, coupled with Wilson's imaginative leadership, made possible an agricultural revolution unmatched by any nation.

By 1900 the American frontier had vanished. Some enlightened conservationists, including President Theodore Roosevelt, realized that much of America's precious natural resources were also vanishing. Little was being done to preserve the nation's soil, forests, waterways, or mineral resources. In 1907 President Roosevelt appointed the Inland Waterways Commission to study flood conditions on the lower Mississippi River. At the commission's suggestion, Roosevelt called the White House Conservation Conference on May 14, 1908, to study the problem. In 1909 Roosevelt convened the North American Conservation Conference. As a result of TR's efforts, the federal government set aside 234 million acres of forestland for future use.

The following excerpts from Roosevelt's opening address to the White House conference speak well for his understanding of conservation: "We have thoughtlessly, and to a large degree unnecessarily, diminished the resources upon which not only our prosperity but the prosperity of our children and our children's children must always depend.

"The time has come to inquire seriously what will happen when our forests are gone, when the coal, the iron, the oil, and the gas are exhausted, when the soils shall have been still further impoverished and washed into the streams, polluting the rivers, denuding the fields, and obstructing navigation. . . . The time has come for a change. As a people we have the right and the duty . . . to protect ourselves and our children against the wasteful development of our natural resources, whether that waste is caused by the actual destruction of such resources or by making them impossible of development hereafter."

The importance of government involvement in the preservation and wise use of our natural resources was first recognized by Republican leaders. President Benjamin Harrison set aside the first 13 million acres of forest reservations. President Theodore Roosevelt, acting under authority granted by Congress, established the principle of national ownership of forests and reserves.

Roosevelt's chief assistant in conservation was the able and brilliant Gifford Pinchot, the first professional American forester. Serving as chief of the Forest Service of the Department of Agriculture from 1898 to 1910, Pinchot was one of the earliest Americans to sense the interrelationship of man and his natural resources. Pinchot also recognized the importance of education in promoting conservation programs.

"Man does not conquer the earth," Pinchot wrote, "but strives to enter into harmonious relationship with it." A professor of forestry at Yale from 1903 to 1936, he founded the Pinchot School of Forestry and later served as governor of Pennsylvania. President Roosevelt said of him: "Especial credit is due to the initiative, the energy, the devotion to duty, and the farsightedness of Gifford Pinchot, to whom we owe so much of the progress we have already made in handling this matter of the coordination and conservation of natural resources."

The ever present problems of flooding, deforestation, soil exhaustion, mineral depletion, and the new dilemma of toxic waste management all mandate that conservation—the heritage of Theodore Roosevelt and Gifford Pinchot—continues to be a top Republican priority.

C. McVicker

Gifford Pinchot and Conservation

Frederick Seaton was eminently qualified to serve his nation as Secretary of the Interior. An editor and Republican leader from a farm state, Nebraska, he served as Secretary of the Interior under Eisenhower from 1956 to 1961. Seaton fully appreciated the need to protect and develop our national parks, monuments, and historical shrines so that they would be available for the enjoyment and inspiration of present and future generations. Immediately upon his appointment as Secretary of the Interior, Seaton implemented the congressionally approved Mission 66. This was the first comprehensive, long-range program to assure the American people that their natural and historical heritage would be properly restored and preserved.

Mission 66 sought to staff, equip, and develop the national parks and other areas administered by the National Park Service in order to meet the anticipated needs of 1966—the golden anniversary of the national park system. The park system had seriously eroded during World War II and was unprepared for the 50 million visitors that appeared in 1956. Ten years later, thanks to Mission 66, that decline had been reversed.

The degree of the program's success can be measured in numbers: 89 million visitors had been forecast for the park system in 1966, yet the system was able to handle all 133 million people who actually visited the parks and wilderness areas.

The accomplishments of Mission 66 were vital to our country: An understanding of our national legacy contributes to the quality of life for all Americans. The goal of safeguarding our natural and historical heritage remains an important Republican concern.

Contributions to
Education and Science

Republican Congressman Justin S. Morrill of Vermont sponsored the Land-Grant Act, which was passed by Congress and signed by President Lincoln on July 2, 1862. The act, since known as the Morrill Act, granted to every state and territory 30,000 acres of public land for each senator and representative the state or territory had in Congress. The law stipulated that the land was to be sold, the proceeds invested, and the income used either to endow a new college of agriculture and mechanical arts or to maintain an existing school. Iowa was the first state to make application for a land-grant college, and Michigan was the first state to have one.

The Morrill Act symbolized the recognition on the part of the Republican-controlled Congress of the need for higher educational institutions to provide the research necessary for America's expanding agriculture. A total of 11,367,832 acres of land was received by the states, and 59 land-grant colleges were established.

Recent decades have brought increased attention to the need for quality educational programs in science and engineering. As at other institutions, academic programs at the land-grant colleges have been broadened in accordance with the developing requirements of modern society. It is impossible to place a monetary value on the educational advances that have resulted from the land-grant system. The land-grant colleges now enroll about 20 percent of the nation's undergraduates and confer nearly 40 percent of all doctoral degrees in every field of study. Their contribution to American life is one of which we all can be proud.

The Atomic Energy Commission was created by the Atomic Energy Act of 1946. The act gave control of the U.S. atomic energy program to a five-member civilian board of commissioners appointed by the President. The Atomic Energy Commission's duties were made clear: "Subject at all times to the paramount objective of assuring the common defense and security, the development and utilization of atomic energy shall, so far as practicable, be directed toward improving the public welfare, increasing the standard of living, strengthening free competition in private enterprise, and promoting world peace."

Lewis L. Strauss was one of the first five commissioners appointed by President Harry S. Truman. Strauss, a New York financier, had begun his public service career in 1917, when he served without pay as Herbert Hoover's private secretary. During World War II he rose to the rank of rear admiral in the Navy and was awarded the Distinguished Service Medal, the Legion of Merit (three awards), and France's Legion of Honor. In 1953 President Eisenhower appointed Strauss chairman of the Atomic Energy Commission. Under his leadership, the commission cooperated with international agencies for the peaceful study of atomic energy and began demonstrating the technical feasibility of generating electricity from atomic energy.

Strauss was a man with high motives and keen insights. From his own words we get a feeling of assurance toward the future: "We stand at the threshold of an era when it will be possible for man to abdicate both the right and responsibility of free decision and to delegate it to the machine." But, he added, though "Machines will be able to determine the means and avenues to goals . . . men will continue to set the goals themselves."

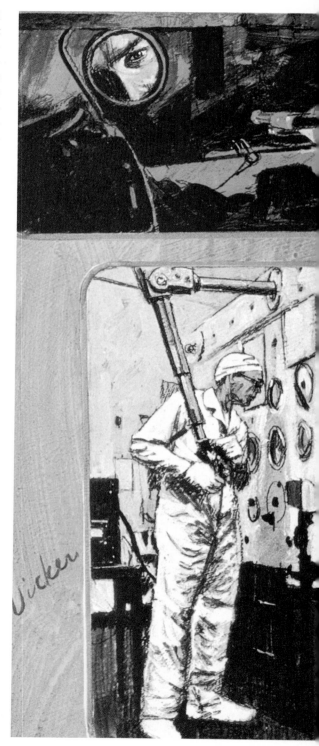

Lewis L. Strauss and Atomic Energy

Eisenhower and the Peaceful Use of the Atom

Under President Dwight D. Eisenhower's leadership, the United States moved into the forefront of the peaceful use of atomic energy. In a major policy speech to the General Assembly of the United Nations, on December 8, 1953, President Eisenhower called for an international "atoms for peace" program aimed at establishing an International Atomic Energy Agency. Such an international body would be empowered to administer the peaceful use of atomic energy and prevent the diversion of atomic projects to military use.

As a result of Eisenhower's efforts, the United States became a member of the International Atomic Energy Agency, created in 1957 and based in Vienna, Austria. The United States also entered into a research agreement with the European Atomic Energy Community (Euratom) and into approximately 50 agreements with individual nations for peaceful atomic energy cooperation.

Our nation never stood taller or appeared more unselfish than when President Eisenhower spoke for us and to the world on atomic energy sharing. These excerpts from his United Nations speech make us proud of this Republican leader and of the United States: "My country wants to be constructive. It wants agreements, not wars among nations. . . . My country's purpose is to help us move out of the dark chambers of horror into the light. . . . The coming months will be fraught with fateful decisions. In this Assembly; in the capitals and military headquarters of the world; in the hearts of men everywhere, be they governors or governed, may they be the decisions which will lead this world out of fear and into peace. . . . To the making of these fateful decisions, the United States pledges before you—and therefore before the world— its determination to help solve the fearful atomic dilemma—to devote its entire heart and mind to find the way by which the miraculous inventiveness of man shall not be dedicated to his death, but consecrated to his life."

Contributions to
Transportation and Commerce

The completion of the first transcontinental railroad was the realization of a great dream. Progress—the urge to move forward, to expand—has always been an American characteristic. So that America could utilize and benefit from its vast expanse of territory, our nation's leaders used the resources of government to encourage traffic on the sea and on rivers, on the land, and finally in the air.

After the advent of the steam engine and its application to travel, early industrialists quickly realized its potential for commerce. Soon great corporations were formed to build and operate a railroad system. As the West began to open, the advantages of a coast-to-coast railroad became obvious. The bill that made this possible was signed by Abraham Lincoln on July 1, 1862.

The completion of the Union Pacific Railroad, which joined the Central Pacific to form a link of steel reaching from the Atlantic to the Pacific, was hailed as a great milestone. The former governor of California and president of the Central Pacific Railroad Company, Leland Stanford, drove home the golden spike at Promontory, Utah, on May 10, 1869. The whole country rejoiced with President Grant when news of the railroad's completion was flashed across the continent by telegraph.

Besides its role in promoting the transcontinental railroad, Republican leadership has helped make possible the construction of countless locks and dams, our national airline system, and the thousands of miles of the Interstate Highway System and its predecessor, the Federal/State System of Roads. These and other accomplishments have provided America with transportation facilities unsurpassed by those of any other country.

C. McVicker

John Hay and the Panama Canal

In 1899 the United States Congress authorized a commission to survey possible interocean canal routes in Latin America. During the Spanish-American War the battleship U.S.S. *Oregon* had to sail nearly 13,000 miles when it was ordered from San Francisco to Cuba—rather than the 4,600 miles had there been a canal through the Isthmus of Panama. This fact emphasized the need for such a canal. In 1903 President Theodore Roosevelt's Secretary of State, John Hay, signed a treaty with the newly recognized Republic of Panama. The treaty gave the United States exclusive control over a ten-mile-wide strip of land through the Isthmus and also guaranteed the independence of the Republic of Panama.

In 1907 Col. George W. Goethals was placed in charge of the canal project. More than 43,000 men worked on the project, moving about 184 million cubic yards of rock and earth. Among those who played a major role in the construction of the canal was Col. William C. Gorgas, Surgeon General of the U.S. Army. Gorgas solved the problems of disease plaguing the project, gaining fame by wiping out yellow fever. The main work on the canal was finished in 1914, with the first passenger-cargo ship, the S.S. *Ancon*, completing the trip through the canal on August 15, 1914.

According to terms included in the purchase of the Canal Zone, the United States provided that the canal would be made available to all the world on an equal basis, and that American vessels would pay the same fee as the vessels of any other nation. The total cost of the canal to the United States was 380 million dollars. Its value to the world, and the true nature of our motives in constructing the canal, were reflected in the motto of the Canal Zone: "The land divided, the world united."

George Dondero and the St. Lawrence Seaway

Following the discovery of North America, adventurers and explorers began to seek a waterway through the continent. It was soon learned that the St. Lawrence River, discovered by Jacques Cartier in 1535 and linking the Atlantic with the Great Lakes, offered the best access to the rich interior of the continent. Beginning in the 1700s, the river was improved to accommodate ever larger vessels. By the 1930s, the St. Lawrence channel had been improved to a depth of 21 to 25 feet. But even this was insufficient to meet the needs of ocean-going traffic.

Farmers, exporters, and political leaders in the United States and in Canada called for increased improvement of the St. Lawrence, but a U.S.-Canadian treaty signed in 1932 was rejected by the U.S. Senate in 1934. Not until 1953 was an agreement reached for the joint construction of the St. Lawrence Seaway. With a minimum depth of 27 feet and a length of 2,350 miles, the project was intended both to improve navigation and to supply water power.

Officially opened by President Eisenhower and Queen Elizabeth on June 26, 1959, the seaway was a tribute to the perseverance of Republican Congressman George Dondero of Michigan. Mr. Dondero's contributions to the seaway were substantial and are in the record. Said a fellow congressman: "He has made a valiant battle for this particular seaway project for many, many years . . . the name of George Dondero should be inscribed at the top of the emblem signifying the project. Your people should say to you, Congressman Dondero, 'A job well done.'"

The Interstate Highway System is an awesome engineering feat, one of which Americans can be proud. All Americans have benefited more from the 100 billion dollar investment in the highway system than from any other investment except that in our educational system. The documented value of the benefits already totals some 500 billion dollars. Some of the benefits include savings in fuel achieved by eliminating stops and starts for buses, cars, and trucks. And there is a staggering savings of time in driving on our modern roads.

Shortly after President Eisenhower was inaugurated in 1953, recommendations were made to him to accelerate construction of the Interstate Highway System. All the necessary preliminary studies and legislation had been put in place through the foresight of Thomas MacDonald of Iowa, who retired in 1953 as Commissioner of Public Roads after 34 years service. At the suggestion of Francis S. DuPont, MacDonald's successor, President Eisenhower appointed a citizens' committee, headed by Gen. Lucius Clay, to make recommendations for the completion of the Interstate Highway System.

Congress received the commission's report and gave it thorough consideration. After the Public Works Subcommittee held 74 days of hearings, a bill was voted out for congressional consideration. Following extensive hearings in the Senate, the bill to build the system was passed and signed by President Eisenhower on June 29, 1956. As a member of Congress from Iowa and a member of the Subcommittee on Roads and Highways, the author witnessed and participated in the birth of the Interstate and Defense Highway Act. Now, 30 years later, the 43,000 miles of the planned highway system have been built and are being used. The investment in the nation's highway system will continue to return dividends for decades to come.

President Calvin Coolidge expressed the belief that his party was a worthy successor to the economic traditions and principles of the Federalists and Whigs. On one occasion he wrote that "manufacturing was the motive power of American civilization. The driving force of American progress has been her industries and technology. They have created the wealth that has wrought our national developments . . . without them the great force of agriculture would now be where it was in the 18th century."

Coolidge saw William McKinley, an outspoken champion of industry, as a worthy successor to Alexander Hamilton, Washington's famous Secretary of the Treasury. Coolidge believed that McKinley had taken up "the work of Hamilton and Clay . . . reestablished their principles," and under his leadership, the government had readopted conservative economic principles.

Under McKinley's administration, and since, we have benefited from what the author has called "the fifth great freedom"—the freedom of movement of men and goods. While America's economic system has been termed the capitalist or profit system, it is more accurately described as the free enterprise system. Our history reveals that while free enterprise at times has served selfish interests, it has most often served the public interest. This is revealed by the fact that the United States, with only 7 percent of the world's land area and less than 5 percent of the world population, has the capacity to produce about a quarter of the world's wealth.

One reason for the success of the free enterprise system is that it is responsive to the public. No other system places so high a premium upon individual responsibility, merit, and leadership. Yet no other system comes close to providing the satisfaction of human needs and wants that the fifth great freedom, free enterprise, has achieved.

Free Enterprise—the Fifth Great Freedom

The Republican Commitment to Labor

"Labor is prior to and independent of capital . . . capital is only the fruit of labor." These are the words of Abraham Lincoln, the first Republican President. They reveal that Republicans, from the very inception of the party, were concerned with labor. That Republicans have a genuine and sincere interest in the problems of the laboring man is made clear by the concerns of Republican leaders: the abolition of slavery, passage of child labor laws and many other labor laws, legislation for shorter hours and the prevailing wage principle, creation of the Labor Department as a Cabinet post.

The late 19th century, the period of industry's most rapid growth, brought with it certain evils and abuses and a lack of concern both for the public interest and the interests of labor. Leaders such as Republican Governor Charles Evans Hughes of New York recognized the problems and resolved to contend with them. Under the guiding hand of Governor Hughes, 54 labor laws were passed by the New York Legislature. These set the pattern used by the other states in the solution of their own labor problems.

When Governor Hughes completed his last term, *Legislative News*, a New York labor publication, said that he was responsible for "many of the best laws ever enacted in this or any other state," and that "he was the greatest friend of labor laws that ever occupied the governor's chair."

Through the years, Republicans have compiled a solid labor record. Today they are still concerned about the problems of the laborer, just as they are concerned about the problems of all the people.

Contributions to
Diplomacy and World Peace

The Nobel Peace Prize represents a worthy recognition of attempts to enhance the prospect for international peace. Since 1901, the Nobel prize has been awarded to more Americans than to citizens of any other single country. Americans can be justly proud of those whose contributions have been recognized; Republicans can be proud that six of the eight American political figures to win the prize have been identified with the Grand Old Party. Republicans who have won the prize include Theodore Roosevelt (1905), Elihu Root (1912), Frank B. Kellogg (1929), Nicholas Murray Butler (1931), Charles G. Dawes (1935), and Henry Kissinger (1973).

President Roosevelt's mediation of the Russo-Japanese War earned him the Nobel Peace Prize. One of the first political leaders to sense the United States' role as a world power, and our concomitant responsibility to promote world peace, Roosevelt persuaded Russia and Japan to agree to the Treaty of Portsmouth, which brought the war to an end. As a result of his efforts, Roosevelt was widely hailed as a peacemaker.

Republican contributions to international peace furnish proof that the party is committed not only to the United States' enduring objective—to safeguarding our own way of life—but also to promoting liberty, well-being, and progress for all mankind. The spirit and dedication of the patriots and statesmen who have been recognized for their efforts toward peace have led the way. In the nuclear age, Republicans remain committed to the search for ways to bring harmony out of discord.

C. McVicker

Taft and the Pan-American Union

The history of the attempts to establish an organization of the nations of North and South America stretches as far back as the early 19th century and the efforts of Venezuelan patriot and liberator Simon Bolivar. Henry Clay, as Secretary of State in the 1820s, was dedicated to the Pan-American idea, but it was not until the late 1800s that an international organization was established.

In 1881, Republican James G. Blaine, then Secretary of State, proposed a conference of the American republics to promote the arbitration and peaceful settlement of international controversies. Thirteen nations sent delegates to the conference, held in Washington, D.C., in 1889-90. As a result, the International Union of American Republics was founded, the oldest international political organization of which the United States has been a member.

The International Union did not become an effective instrument for peace until the 20th century. In 1910 its name was changed to the Pan-American Union. The organization's objectives remained the same—to promote a better understanding of Pan-American problems and to enhance the cause of peace. The headquarters, located in Washington, contain the largest collection of information on intercontinental relationships to be found anywhere. Since its organization, the Union has held many important conferences and developed many successful programs.

The Pan-American Union, now known as the Organization of American States, today represents 32 member countries. Like the Tree of Peace, planted in ceremonies by President William Howard Taft, relationships among members have steadily continued to grow and improve.

Few Americans' contributions to their nation and the world have been as great as those of Nicholas Murray Butler. A quiet, dignified scholar, Butler had a zeal for education and the international rule of law that animated his entire career. So renowned was his expertise as an educator that before he reached his late 30s he had been offered the presidencies of the state universities of Ohio, Indiana, Illinois, Wisconsin, Iowa, Colorado, Washington, and California. Butler, however, was devoted to transforming his alma mater, Columbia, into a major university. In 1902, he became president of Columbia, a position he retained until 1945, just two years before his death.

Shortly after the turn of the century, Butler began a crusade for world peace through international arbitration. As president of the Lake Mohonk (New York) Conference on International Arbitration in 1907, 1909, 1910 and 1911, he persuaded Andrew Carnegie to establish the Carnegie Endowment for International Peace, set up in 1911. A trustee of the foundation from its outset, Butler served as its president from 1925 to 1945. In 1931, he shared the Nobel Peace Prize with Jane Addams for their work on behalf of peace.

A stalwart Republican his entire life, Butler allowed his name to be substituted for that of vice presidential candidate James S. Sherman, who died shortly before the 1912 election. Butler's observations on world peace remain cogent today: "The problem of the One and the Many lies at the bottom of all logic, of all ethics, of all economics, and of all politics; it lies at the bottom of the problem of nationalism and internationalism . . . a nation exists not for self-aggrandizement but for the promotion of the general good, and that it may grow great and strong and rich without danger to mankind."

Nicholas Murray Butler and World Peace

Contributions to
American Government

The Campaign and the Two-Party System

As William Howard Taft traveled by train across America in 1908, shaking hands and making speeches, he was taking part in a great American political tradition: the campaign. The ritual of two or more candidates of rival political parties publicly contesting for the people's vote is more than a colorful spectacle. It is an indispensable mechanism for democratic self-government. As Queen Wilhelmina of the Netherlands observed before a joint session of Congress in 1942: "Seeing this [government] . . . renewing itself at regular intervals . . . under self-made rules of law, seems to me a sure guarantee that liberty is forever young and strong and invincible."

American history has seen many kinds of campaigns. At first, presidential candidates did not campaign for their own elections—even while a candidate for President, Lincoln made no campaign speeches. Since that time, however, a great variety of campaign techniques have been used, including direct campaigning, stump-speaking, and debates. Gimmicks and gadgets have enlivened political races, including buttons, posters, pictures, and publications of all kinds. When the railroad became popular, campaigning from trains provided an opportunity to meet and plead with a larger segment of the population. Now we have advanced to the use of the airplane, radio, and television, with millions of dollars spent in every national election.

It has always been an objective of the Republican Party to improve the level of political campaigning and to strengthen the character of the electorate. America needs more discerning voters, men and women who are informed, understanding, and reasonable. "We are acting for all mankind," Jefferson said in 1802, and it is as true today, for when we vote we act for posterity as well as for ourselves.

The Party's Dedication to Law and Order

In the 1850s, when the Republican Party was organized, justice and the law were in flux. The bloody confrontations in Kansas over the slavery issue and John Brown's raid on Harpers Ferry were but two examples of the breakdown of law and order. At its inception, the Republican Party was dedicated to the rule of law and to clarifying the moral basis of our national conception of justice.

Throughout its history, the Republican Party has produced leaders who have taken a strong stand on law and order. Former Senator Edward W. Brooke was born in Washington, D.C., and educated in the public schools there. He graduated from Howard University in 1941 and studied law at Boston University, graduating in 1949. He also served five years as a captain in the U.S. Army. Serving with distinction as Attorney General of Massachusetts, he was later elected to the U.S. Senate in 1966, where he became highly respected as a legislator.

During his career, Senator Brooke contributed significantly to the building of a better America. In addition to holding public office, he served the public voluntarily in many ways in the private sector. Brooke's reverence for the law is reflected in his statements: "No nation can remain healthy unless people and their property can be made safe—in their homes, on the streets, and in their places of business. . . . Laws and institutions must go hand in hand with the progress of the human mind. . . . Though law has roots which antedate the beginning of recorded history, it can never be a static institution."

Herbert Hoover and the Hoover Commission

C. McVicker

Herbert Hoover, the man from West Branch, Iowa, was described by historian Earl Schenck Miers as "a man and a symbol, [a] dynamo of human energy and an inspiration." He was one of the world's leading engineers and one of its greatest humanitarians. During World War I, he coordinated relief measures in Belgium and served as Food Administrator in the United States. In the '20s he served as Secretary of Commerce during the Harding and Coolidge Administrations. Elected President in 1928, Hoover was overwhelmed by the Great Depression. Wrongly blamed for the Depression, he took steps, including the establishment of the Reconstruction Finance Corporation, to bring about recovery.

During his long and active retirement, Hoover never lost faith in America, as his volumes of writings and speeches indicate so eloquently. His contributions to American government were capped by the two nonpartisan Hoover Commissions he chaired. The first functioned in 1947-49 to deal with the growth of the government during World War II; the second dealt with its growth during the Korean War. The commissions returned 273 and 314 recommendations respectively, about 70 percent of which were put into effect. Among the reforms that resulted were: passage of the Military Unification Act of 1949; creation of the General Services Agency; formation of the Department of Health, Education, and Welfare; cost accounting and modernized budgeting; coordination of federal research; and the reduction of red tape. Hoover himself estimated that the commissions brought savings of more than three billion dollars yearly.

Earl Schenck Miers' evaluation of Hoover rings true: "His devotion to this country and his love for humanity set him apart. He belonged to his age as a man of incorruptible honor and of a sincerity of purpose that relied on God's help and man's wisdom."

Republicans should never lose sight of the contributions women have made to the party, nor the important role women play in its present and future. Though many early Republican leaders favored women's suffrage, it was not until the 20th century that women got the vote—and when they did, Republicans were in the forefront. The first woman elected to Congress was Jeannette Rankin, a Republican from Montana, elected in 1916.

Many of the notable women to serve in Congress have been Republicans: Margaret Chase Smith, Nancy Landon Kassebaum, and Paula Hawkins in the Senate; Frances P. Bolton, Marguerite Stitt Church, Florence P. Dwyer, Millicent Fenwick, Bobbi Fiedler, Mrs. Cecil M. Harden, Margaret Heckler, Marjorie Holt, Florence P. Kahn, Clare Boothe Luce, Lynn Martin, Catherine May, Charlotte T. Reid, Marge Roukema, Edith Nourse Rogers, Claudine Schneider, Katherine St. George, Virginia Smith, Olympia J. Snowe, Jessie Sumner, and Ruth Thompson, among others, in the House. The effectiveness of Republican women legislators is reflected in their own words:

Margaret Chase Smith: "Surely the U.S. Senate is big enough to take self-criticism and self-appraisal. . . . I think it is high time we remember that the Constitution speaks not only for freedom of speech, but also of trial by jury instead of trial by accusation."

Frances P. Bolton: "Foreign aid can never be an adequate substitute for foreign policy."

Catherine May: "When you harness the new awareness and the knowledge that American women have today to political activity, you have a great national force to be reckoned with."

Margaret Heckler: "The Congress can—and must be—the repository of national trust and confidence."

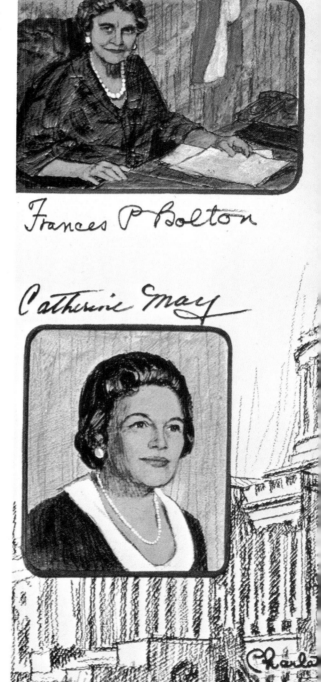

Frances P Bolton

Catherine May

Abraham Lincoln: "My countrymen . . . think calmly and *well*. . . . Nothing valuable can be lost by taking time. . . . We are not enemies, but friends. . . . Fondly do we hope, fervently do we pray, that this mighty scourge of war may speedily pass away."

Andrew Johnson: "The Federal Constitution, the *magna charta* of American rights, under whose wise and salutary provisions we have successfully conducted all our . . . affairs, sustained ourselves in peace and in war, and become a great nation . . ."

Ulysses S. Grant: "The question of suffrage is one which is likely to agitate the public so long as a portion of the citizens of the nation are excluded from its privileges in any State."

Rutherford B. Hayes: "A moral obligation rests upon the National Government . . . to establish the rights of the people it has emancipated."

James A. Garfield: "We cannot overestimate the fervent love of liberty, the intelligent courage, and the sum of common sense with which our fathers made the great experiment of self-government."

Chester A. Arthur: "It seems to me that the time has arrived when the people may justly demand some relief from their present onerous burden, and that by due economy in the various branches of the public service this may readily be afforded."

Benjamin Harrison: "Let us exalt patriotism and moderate our party contentions. . . . A party success that is achieved by unfair methods . . . is hurtful."

William McKinley: "Immunity should be granted to none who violate the laws, whether individuals, corporations, or communities."

Theodore Roosevelt: "Our relations with the other powers of the world are important; but still more important are our relations among ourselves."

William Howard Taft: "Our international policy is always to promote peace. . . . we, of course, shall make every effort consistent with national honor . . . to avoid a resort to arms."

Warren G. Harding: "Americanism must be more than the conservation of the individual. In this great fulfillment, we must have a citizenship less concerned about what the government can do for them and more anxious about what they can do for the nation."

Calvin Coolidge: "I favor the policy of economy, not because I wish to save money, but because I want to save people."

Herbert Hoover: "It is impossible . . . to speak of peace without profound emotion. . . . Surely, civilization is old enough, surely mankind is mature enough so that we ought in our own lifetime to find a way to permanent peace."

Dwight D. Eisenhower: "We look upon this shaken earth, and we declare our firm and fixed purpose—the building of a peace . . . in a world where moral law prevails."

Richard M. Nixon: "We must do . . . a better job of informing the people of why our sound principles are in their best interests. . . . We must make it clear to the people that we are conservative because we believe this is the best way to progress—to produce better jobs, higher wages, better homes, better medical care, more security and all the other good things that people want."

Gerald R. Ford: "I believe more strongly than ever that the House is the institution of government that most accurately and consistently reflects the sentiments and moods of the American people. It truly is a microcosm of the nation."

Ronald Reagan: "All of us together, in and out of government, must bear the burden. . . . Our forbearance should never be misunderstood. Our reluctance for conflict should not be misjudged as a failure of will. When action is required to preserve our national security, we will act."

2
130 Years of Achievement
The Story of the Republican Party

An in-depth look at the party's founding, its triumphs,
and its losses. Accompanied by 53 historical illustrations.

"To be a good Republican you gotta know your history" echoes a statement made by President Harry S. Truman, who said, "You gotta know your history if you want to be a good citizen." When Horace Greeley, Alvan Bovay, and others joined to form a new political party in the 1850s, they had the benefit of American history to help them find an appropriate name. Despite the many possibilities available to them, the party founders settled on a name that recalled memories of the great men and events in the history of this country.

Thomas Jefferson, at his first inaugural, declared, "We are all Republicans, we are all Federalists. . . . Let us then pursue with courage and confidence our own federal and republican principles." Earlier, those who voted to sever ties with England replaced government by hereditary monarchy with a still highly experimental form of government—the *republic*. The delegates to the Constitutional Convention were so concerned with insuring the success of a political system for which so many had fought and died that they wrote a clause into the Constitution guaranteeing a representative form of government in every state. They declared their faith in the good sense of the people; for, in a republic, the people rule.

A few years after the adoption of the Constitution, a growing disagreement over the role of government led to the formation of political parties. With a sense for public relations that would have made a 20th-century advertising man proud, Thomas Jefferson and James Madison called their party by the two words with which most Americans would have identified themselves: Democratic-Republicans. During the following years, this party gained the allegiance of the overwhelming majority of people. Gradually, and probably because the party's name was a bit long, its second half fell into disuse. When opposition rose to the policies of Andrew Jackson, a new party was formed. Led by men such as Henry Clay and John Quincy Adams, this party, too, appealed to the historical con-

sciousness of the electorate when it came to choosing its name: National Republicans.

Soon, however, and for reasons not quite clear, the name "republican" passed from the American political scene, and in its place the Whig Party came into being. But republicanism remained the honored form of government, and in Alvan Bovay's mind, no other name would be appropriate for the new party he and his colleagues envisioned. Thus, in 1854, the Republican Party was born.

A Party and A Principle

Two devastating wars with England and the creation of a strong and stable government were the major concerns of American leaders in the early years of independence. A number of other issues, however, regularly threatened to upset the peaceful growth of the nation. One issue that rose again and again slowly came to be the most important: slavery.

Under the leadership of Thomas Jefferson, slavery had been banned from the "Northwest" even before the Constitution was adopted. Compromises reached during the Constitutional Convention kept the issue from becoming a crisis for many years. Westward expansion brought the question of slavery to the forefront again in 1820, but a compromise in that year and another in 1850 brought a temporary respite.

Many Americans, though, were not satisfied with those compromises. They insisted on the abolition of slavery everywhere in the United States. Two related groups spearheaded the attack on slavery. The first was led by religious figures who insisted that God recognized no differences among men, and therefore, slavery was against the moral law. The second group was composed of those who believed slavery was both morally and politically indefensible. They took their stance from Jefferson: "We hold these truths to be self-evident, that all men are created equal, that they are endowed by the Creator with certain unalienable Rights, that among these are Life, Liberty, and the pursuit of Happiness."

Still, the major case against slavery was a *moral* argument, and it is often difficult to transfer a moral issue into the arena of politics. The first attempt to force slavery into the American political consciousness was made by the Liberty Party. Its creation was at least partly due to the refusal of both major parties—Democrats and Whigs—to allow outspoken opposition to slavery within their ranks. Abolitionists believed that both parties depended too much on their southern supporters for them to endorse freedom for slaves. James G. Birney was the Liberty Party candidate for President in 1840 and again in 1844. Though he did not receive widespread support, in 1844 Birney won enough votes from Whig candidate Henry Clay in New York to give the election to Democrat James K. Polk.

By 1848 the Liberty Party had collapsed, but it was replaced by the Free Soil Party, dedicated to preventing the expansion of slavery into the western territories. Benefiting from the candidacy of former Democratic President Martin Van Buren, the Free Soilers received almost five times as many votes in 1848 as the Liberty Party did four years earlier. Without Van Buren, the vote totals fell off badly in 1852. Both these parties suffered from the refusal of antislavery men in the major parties—the Conscience Whigs and the Barnburner Democrats—to desert to the new parties. However, this would soon change.

Antislavery advocates thought they had hemmed in the "peculiar institution" by the Missouri Compromise of 1820. Under its terms, slavery would not be allowed in America's western territories north of latitude 36°30'—the southern boundary of Missouri. Since all the land controlled by the United States in the west was north of that line, with the exception of the old Indian and Arkansas territories, slavery would be banned forever from most of the country.

Tempers cooled after the Missouri Compromise, but only for a few years. Passions flared again over the question of the annexa-

tion of Texas. The addition of new territory in the Southwest was opposed by antislavery forces because it would nullify the success of the Missouri Compromise: Slavery would once again have room to expand. It was not surprising, then, that the controversy sparked considerable opposition to the war with Mexico over Texas. Among the members of Congress who voted against the declaration of war was an almost unknown freshman representative from Illinois, Abraham Lincoln.

Following the Missouri Compromise, states had been admitted to the Union in pairs—one from the North and one from the South. For many years the population of the North had been growing much more quickly than that of the South. Because seats in the House of Representatives were determined by population, the North commanded a majority of votes there. But in the Senate, every state—regardless of size—had equal representation. Since both houses had to agree in order to pass legislation, the South was able to short-circuit attempts to end slavery by maintaining its Senate equality.

Even with the addition of Texas and the rest of the southwestern lands won from Mexico, not enough slave states could be formed to balance the large free territory destined for statehood. By 1850, as a result of the gold rush, the population of California had grown rapidly, and the territory was ready to become a state. However, there was no new slave state available to keep the balance in the Senate, so the South objected.

At this time Henry Clay, in one of the last great acts of his career, persuaded the South to accept a compromise—the famed Compromise of 1850. The battle over that compromise is remembered as the last confrontation of the Senate's "great triumvirate": Clay, Daniel Webster, and John C. Calhoun, all of whom would die within the following two years. It also marked the emergence to national attention of two men who would become central figures in the soon-to-be-created Republican Party: Salmon P. Chase and William H. Seward.

Gifted orator fashioned by humble beginnings and a yearning for knowledge: Abraham Lincoln began life in a log cabin and years later moved into the White House as the first Republican President of the United States. His eloquence as a speaker and his firm resolve to preserve the Union during the Civil War distinguish Lincoln as one of the nation's greatest Presidents.

Although the final compromise was more complicated, it boiled down to the North receiving a new free state, California, along with the abolition of the slave trade in the District of Columbia. The South, on the other hand, got a strong fugitive slave law, which it had demanded for years. As is true of many compromises, this one satisfied few. It did not settle the controversy over slavery. It only provided a short truce, and Senator Seward was only one of many who recognized this fact. Knowing that both sides in the conflict were firmly convinced their cause was just, he predicted: "It is an irrepressible conflict between opposing and enduring forces, and it means that the United States must and will, sooner or later, become either entirely a slave-holding nation, or entirely a free labor nation."

Meanwhile, the northern states were sending more men to Congress who rejected the Compromise of 1850. They were led, in the House, by Joshua Giddings of Ohio, long a foe of slavery, and, in the Senate, by Charles Sumner, a young Free Soiler who would later become a leading Republican. The antislavery forces kept up a continuing agitation. They were helped mightily by a related event, the publication in 1852 of Harriet Beecher Stowe's antislavery novel, *Uncle Tom's Cabin.*

In the face of agitation, southern proslavery propaganda kept tempers rising. And, once again, westward expansion contributed to the differences between the sections. Settlers were moving into the Great Plains, and there was demand for a railroad that would enable them to market their crops in the East. A railroad also was needed to connect the eastern states with the new settlers on the West Coast. Both North and South wanted the railroad to be built in its section. One Northerner devised a plan he thought would cause the South to accept a railroad in the North. His name was Stephen A. Douglas and his idea became the Kansas-Nebraska Act of 1854.

The Kansas-Nebraska Act provided for the organization of two new territories from the lands of the Louisiana Purchase. Both were north of the line that had divided free and slave territories, but under this act the settlers of the new territories were to decide themselves whether to allow slavery—a doctrine known as "popular sovereignty." Southerners supported Douglas' idea because they expected the southern territory, Kansas, to vote for slavery.

Passage of the Kansas-Nebraska Act caused a breakdown in the existing political system. For years, the slavery issue had been slowly destroying the Whig Party, and now the party collapsed. Similarly, many antislavery Democrats had felt increasingly uncomfortable in a party dominated by southern slaveholders. For some of them, Stephen Douglas' idea was the last straw. Unhappy Northerners of the existing parties began to join together, rallying around the principle that there should be no slavery in the western territories. The founders of this movement had been Free Soilers, Conscience Whigs, or Barnburner Democrats. Soon they were to be united as Republicans.

Founding Fathers and First Successes

New political parties do not just spring up overnight, and the Republican Party was no exception. It took hard work by a number of men to accomplish the difficult task. Sometimes they worked independently and sometimes together, but always the goal was the same: uniting all the foes of slavery. The first stirrings toward the party's formation came from the Middle West. Traditionally, the Republican Party traces its origins to February 28, 1854, when the Whig reformer Alvan Bovay called a meeting at Ripon, Wisconsin, to oppose the expansion of slavery into the western territories. Similar meetings took place elsewhere.

The first high-placed figure to attach himself to the movement was Salmon P. Chase, an old foe of slavery though he was not yet 50 years old. Chase had been a leader of Ohio's antislavery movement. During the

1840s he had written platforms for both the state and national Liberty Party. In 1849 he became a United States senator, elected by a coalition ticket of Democrats and Free Soilers. Just three months after the Ripon meeting, Chase delivered one of his most famous speeches, the "Appeal of the Independent Democrats." In this speech Chase called for rejection of the Kansas-Nebraska Act because it was an "enormous crime."

A few weeks later another illustrious voice joined the chorus of opposition to blind adherence to the doctrines of the traditional parties. Horace Greeley was the famous and influential editor of the New York *Tribune*, and a power in Whig politics. In an editorial, he stressed that he remained a firm believer in the principles of the Whig Party. But he recognized that the Free Soilers shared those principles, and he called for a union of the supporters of both parties. The name for this new party, he wrote, was not important—but "Republican" would properly describe the people who wanted "to restore our Union to its true mission—of champion and promulgator of Liberty rather than propagandist of slavery."

Chase and Greeley had been encouraged to take their public positions by the action of a group of congressmen. Representative Israel Washburn of Maine—one of four brothers who had illustrious careers representing four different states in Congress—called a meeting at which 30 members of Congress agreed to form a new party.

In mid-summer of 1854, the first concrete action was taken toward forming an antislavery party. On July 6, a mass meeting was held at Jackson, Michigan, by citizens who refused to accept the old parties' unwillingness to take a firm stand against slavery. They called themselves Republicans, organized a formal party, adopted a platform, and nominated a full slate of candidates for state offices. Other states quickly followed the Michigan example, and the Republican Party spread through the North.

No great political party can rely on a single issue, no matter how important. Had the Republicans stood only for an end to slavery, the party probably would have had a short life, even if successful. Almost by chance, many of the antislavery founders of the Republican Party shared other beliefs, including the support of homesteading in the West, larger government expenditures on internal improvements to ease the opening of the West, and high tariffs to protect America's infant industries. Nevertheless, the overriding issue in the early years was slavery.

The new party got off to a rousing start, recording a series of victories in 1854. Maine and Michigan elected Republican governors. In coalition with a number of other parties opposed to various Democratic policies, the Republicans prevented the Democrats from carrying a single northern state. No party gained a majority in Congress, but the Republicans composed a large minority. Included in this group were several men already famous, or soon to become famous, as congressional leaders: three of the Washburn brothers, future Speaker of the House and Vice President Schuyler Colfax, future Speaker Galusha Grow, John Sherman, and Joshua Giddings. With the large number of parties represented in Congress, the fight to elect a Speaker was long and hard. The eventual winner was a Republican, Nathaniel Banks.

Many leading foes of slavery, however, were not yet ready to desert their old parties. Senator William Seward of New York remained a Whig, as did a losing senatorial candidate from Illinois—Abraham Lincoln. But events of 1855 and 1856 convinced most of the holdouts to transfer to the new party. The most important of those events was guerrilla warfare in Kansas. Friends and foes of slavery were sending large numbers of settlers into the territory, trying to establish a majority that would lead to a territorial government favorable to their position. Frequently the two groups clashed, and the territory earned the name "Bleeding Kansas."

Both sides in the Kansas struggle created governments and wrote constitutions, but Democratic President Franklin Pierce recog-

On February 28, 1854, Whigs, Free Soilers, and Democrats came to this schoolhouse in Ripon, Wisconsin, to attend an antislavery meeting. By the time they adjourned, the delegates had formed the Republican Party. Among their goals was to fight the spread of slavery into the western territories of the United States.

nized the pro-slavery faction as the true government, and fighting continued. Then Republican Senator Charles Sumner of Massachusetts made a rather abusive speech that included a personal attack on a southern senator, Andrew Butler. Representative Preston Brooks, Butler's nephew, was so enraged at Sumner's words that he beat him over the head with a cane on the Senate floor, forcing Sumner to spend many months in the hospital. The result was even greater anger toward slaveholders and increased popularity for the Republican Party.

Republicans continued to make great political strides throughout the northern states. By the beginning of 1856 the number of Republican governors had increased to four, and five others had been elected by coalitions which included Republicans. The new session of Congress that year included over one hundred Republicans in the House, in addition to 15 senators. Meanwhile, the Whig Party collapsed and the Know-Nothings, a party based on opposition to immigration, was quickly

Emotions explode on the Senate floor as Representative Preston Brooks of South Carolina canes Republican Senator Charles Sumner of Massachusetts in May 1856. The attack came after Sumner had given Brooks' uncle, Senator Andrew P. Butler of South Carolina, an abusive tongue-lashing for advocating slavery in the Kansas territory. The beating put Sumner in the hospital for many months and won sympathy and increased popularity for the Republican Party.

fading. The Republicans absorbed most of the following of both parties.

As a result of these gains, Republican prospects were bright when it came time to nominate a candidate for the presidential election of 1856. The Democrats nominated James Buchanan. Among Republicans, radicals and moderates on the question of slavery disagreed on who to nominate. They finally agreed on the candidacy of a man whose political principles were not well known, but who was one of the heroes of the age—John C. Frémont. Frémont had won the nickname the "Pathfinder" for his explorations of the West and for his participation in the liberation of California from Mexico.

Early in 1856, Frémont presented his views on the question central to all Republicans. "I am opposed to slavery on principle . . . and am inflexibly opposed to its extension on this continent beyond its present limits." Frémont won the Republican nomination easily, and the party's platform plank on slavery essentially followed his moderate position. The platform insisted that slavery not be allowed in the territories, but said nothing about the status of slavery elsewhere and ignored the widely hated Fugitive Slave Law.

Financial issues were ignored because of the differences between former Whigs and former Democrats, but there was unanimous support for federal aid in the building of a transcontinental railroad and other internal improvements. Abraham Lincoln, though he did not attend the convention, was the second choice for Vice President, according to an informal ballot. The convention adjourned chanting the battle cry of the Frémont campaign: "Free Soil, Free Labor, Free Speech, Free Men, Frémont!"

The 1856 campaign became a three-way race when remnants of the Whig and Know-Nothing Parties that refused to support Frémont created the American Party and nominated former President Millard Fillmore. It was a curious election in a number of ways. For one thing, the candidates all used different vocabularies, hoping to increase their appeal by recalling the glories of the past. The Americans talked about their faith in the Constitution and the importance of unity. Democrats talked about the Monroe Doctrine and popular sovereignty. Republicans stressed the Declaration of Independence and the Northwest Ordinance, both documents that clearly opposed slavery.

Frémont was not even on the ballot in 14 southern and border states; he was clearly a northern candidate. In one southern state, South Carolina, there was no popular vote—Buchanan electors were chosen by the state legislature. Fillmore won only one state, Maryland. Frémont carried 12 northern states, losing only in Illinois, Indiana, New Jersey, and Buchanan's home state of Pennsylvania. But those four northern states and the 13 southern states were enough to give the Democrats the victory.

Losing is always disheartening, but the Republicans had good reason to be pleased this time. The party was barely two years old, and yet it had been able to get a third of the total vote. Even better, in the states where

slavery was illegal, Frémont had received more votes than Buchanan. And best of all, these were the states that had the most rapidly growing populations, so they would become more important in later elections.

Others also saw that the Republicans had a great future. Some were people who had admitted earlier that they shared Republican principles, but rather than switching allegiances, they had hoped their own parties would adopt those principles. Whig Senator William Seward of New York had been one of those, but he overcame his reluctance to desert his old party as it began to crumble around him. Another who hesitated was Abraham Lincoln. Lincoln's principles certainly were the same as those of the Republicans, but he found it difficult to support Frémont when there was still a Whig in the running. On the other hand, he could not support Fillmore on a platform that accepted slavery. It took much soul-searching before Lincoln could turn to the Republican Party.

In 1857 many took the same step that Lincoln had taken, and not only because of the Whig Party's collapse. This was to become a pivotal year for the nation. Just two days after James Buchanan became President, the Supreme Court issued one of its most famous and controversial opinions. The case involved a slave name Dred Scott. Scott had been the property of an army surgeon, and had accompanied his master on tours of duty in the free states of Illinois and Iowa and the free territory of Minnesota. Both men returned to their original home, Missouri, and there the surgeon died. Somewhat later Scott sued for his freedom on the ground that residence in a free territory made him a free man. The Missouri courts ruled against him, but a complicated legal situation led to federal appeals.

The Dred Scott case could not be separated from the political climate of the time, and the Supreme Court chose to use the opportunity to rule on the larger question of the legality of slavery in the territories. The Court's decision was never really in doubt—seven of the nine justices were Democrats, and five were from

Negro slave Dred Scott sued for his freedom in 1857, claiming that the residency he had briefly spent on free soil made him a free man. Not so, said the U.S. Supreme Court, which took the occasion to add that Congress had no power to exclude slavery from the territories and that the Missouri Compromise of 1820 was therefore unconstitutional. The controversial ruling prompted more citizens to join the Republican Party in the hope of abolishing slavery.

the South. Nine separate opinions were presented, but five were very similar.

Included in that group was the opinion of Chief Justice Roger B. Taney. Taney and his colleagues announced two basic principles. The first was that no black could qualify as a citizen. Constitutionally, Taney reasoned, blacks had no rights that white men were bound to respect. This meant that Scott, who was not a citizen under Missouri law, did not have the right to sue. The second principle was that slaves were property, and since the Fifth Amendment prohibited Congress from taking property without due process of law, Congress could not prevent slave owners from moving their property into any territory.

Antislavery people were outraged at this decision. Republicans were particularly upset because Taney's second principle meant that their party platform—no extension of slavery into the territories—was now unconstitutional. Not surprisingly, Republicans refused to accept this decision. Instead, they threatened to ''pack'' the court with new antislavery justices when they gained control of the government; the victory for the slave forces was destined to be short-lived.

Other events in 1857 strengthened the appeal of the Republican Party. President Buchanan, under southern pressure, recommended that Kansas be admitted to the Union as a slave state. Since Kansans had first accepted, then rejected, a pro-slavery constitution, Buchanan's decision seemed to be a repudiation of the policy of popular sovereignty. Senator Douglas broke with his party over this issue, causing a deadlock on the statehood vote as well as serious division among the Democrats. The year also saw an economic slump develop, causing businessmen and western farmers to look favorably at the Republicans, who recommended higher tariffs, internal improvements, and low-cost homestead legislation.

In 1858, the Republican Party continued its growth. Although the party still did not have a majority in the House of Representatives, it had the largest representation, and a Republican, William Pennington of New Jersey, was elected Speaker. Twenty-five Republicans had been elected to the Senate, and 12 had won governorships. But in the most famous race—one that was a preliminary to the presidential campaign of 1860—the Republican candidate suffered defeat. This important contest took place in Illinois.

Lincoln-Douglas Debates

Senator Stephen Douglas, long a Democratic leader and a contender for his party's presidential nomination, was up for reelection and fighting for his political life. To oppose him, the Republicans put forth Abraham Lincoln. At the convention that nominated him, Lincoln gave one of his greatest speeches: "A house divided against itself cannot stand. I believe this government cannot endure, permanently half *slave* and half *free*. I do not expect the Union to be *dissolved*—I do not expect the house to *fall*—but I *do* expect it will cease to be divided. It will become *all* one thing, or *all* the other." It was obvious to all on which side Lincoln stood.

Stephen Douglas was one of the best-known men in America. Realizing he was the underdog, Lincoln challenged Douglas to a series of seven debates around the state. Douglas accepted, and the meeting between the "Little Giant" and the "Rail-Splitter" gained nationwide attention. At each debate, thousands of people gathered to listen. The voters were treated to an in-depth discussion of the key issue—the extension of slavery. Douglas spoke in favor of popular sovereignty, charging Lincoln with promoting a war between the sections and accusing him of favoring social equality of whites and blacks. Lincoln denied both those charges and accused his opponent of ignoring the moral issue when he advocated popular sovereignty. In fact, both men were against social and political equality of the races, and both opposed the extension of slavery into the territories. But Lincoln insisted on calling slavery a wrong, while Douglas refused to go that far.

Politically and historically, the most important debate was the one that took place at Freeport on August 26, 1858. Lincoln asked Douglas a question that put him on the spot: Was popular sovereignty still a legal formula, now that the Supreme Court's Dred Scott decision ruled it illegal for Congress to prevent slavery in the territories? The question caught Douglas "between the devil and the deep blue sea." If Douglas insisted on his position that territories could reject slavery, southern Democrats would be furious and probably prevent his presidential nomination in 1860. But if he accepted the pro-slavery stance represented by the Dred Scott decision, he would anger Illinois voters and lose the Senate race to Lincoln.

To his credit, Douglas did not duck the issue, and his answer has become known as the Freeport Doctrine. According to Douglas, popular sovereignty would still work. If the people of a territory opposed slavery they could prevent its introduction simply by refusing to pass laws recognizing the right to own slaves. The answer was good enough to win the Senate seat for Douglas, but only because Illinois was gerrymandered so that a narrow Republican majority of the popular vote turned into a narrow Democratic majority in the state legislature.

Lincoln's defeat barely slowed the Republican advance. In the long run it might have helped the party. The debates gave Lincoln national recognition, and the Freeport Doctrine was not acceptable to many Northerners who were not yet Republican. Similarly, a number of Republican defeats in Congress in late 1858 and 1859 probably benefited the new party. Southern votes, or Buchanan vetoes, blocked Republican demands for a higher tariff, a transcontinental railroad, a homestead bill, and aid in the creation of land-grant colleges—all popular measures among Northerners.

Events in the year or so before the 1860 election made it certain the contest would revolve around the question of slavery. One was

"Have we ever had any peace on this slavery question?" asks Abraham Lincoln during a debate in 1858 with Stephen A. Douglas over the question of the Supreme Court's ruling on slavery. The Republicans had picked Lincoln to run against Douglas for the U.S. Senate. Lincoln lost the election due to redistricting, but his impressive showing against Douglas in the series of seven debates in Illinois gained him a national reputation and made him a presidential contender.

the publication of a book. Just as *Uncle Tom's Cabin* had roused the North a few years earlier, Hinton Helper's *The Impending Crisis of the South* now excited the South. Helper was a Southerner who attacked slavery on the ground that it retarded the economic development of the South and benefited wealthy slave owners at the expense of the white masses. He suggested that yeoman farmers overthrow slavery in their own interest.

Enraged Southerners tried to prevent circulation of Helper's book, with much success, since southern postmasters refused to deliver it. But southern leaders were worried. What if the Republicans appointed new postmasters who insisted on delivering not only Helper's book but abolitionist material as well?

For slave owners an even more ominous development was John Brown's raid on Harpers Ferry. The abolitionist fanatic had attacked a federal arsenal in an attempt to obtain guns to arm slaves and start a revolt. Though Brown was captured, convicted, and put to death, Southerners feared abolitionists would make other such attempts, and that one might succeed. Mistakenly, slave owners considered all Republicans abolitionists. What would happen they wondered, if the Republicans won the upcoming election?

The Election of 1860

During the 1858 Illinois Senate race a young newspaperman named James G. Blaine made a prediction that was widely ridiculed: "The State will go for Douglas. He will be elected Senator: but Lincoln will be the next President." Two years later Blaine, now a Republican member of Maine's House of Representatives, was present when Lincoln was notified of his nomination for the Presidency. Lincoln turned to him and said, "Young man, you see I have kept your prediction."

No one will ever know if Lincoln expected that prediction to come true. We do know, however, that his path to the White House was not an easy one. The first hurdle facing Lincoln was the other candidates for the nomination. There were a number of possibilities. New York Senator William Seward was the early favorite. He was the best-known man in the party and had been a foe of slavery for many years. In fact, during the 1858 New York campaign he had described the argument between North and South as an "irrepressible conflict."

But it was just this prominence that destroyed Seward's chances: People identified him as being radical on the question of slavery (though he actually was not). And the Republicans wanted someone moderate enough to

appeal to ex-Whigs who still hadn't committed themselves to Republicanism. The same problem helped defeat the chances of Ohioan Salmon Chase. Age worked against former Whig Edward Bates, and Simon Cameron could not develop enough support. The Republican nominating convention met in Chicago and, though Seward led on the first two ballots, Lincoln won on the third.

Lincoln's success probably surprised Seward and the other contenders, but it was the result of careful campaigning. It was also helped by the Republicans' desire to put forth a candidate who had made few enemies. What was perhaps Lincoln's most important preconvention speech—and among the most notable speeches of his career—took place at Cooper Union in New York City in February 1860. Though the debates with Douglas had given Lincoln some recognition, his New York appearance would launch him as a truly national figure. A recent Senate speech by Seward had disappointed many of his followers because it concentrated on economic rather that moral differences between the northern and southern labor systems. This gave Lincoln the opportunity to preempt the moral issue.

Lincoln's carefully crafted presentation emphasized that both he and his party were moderate, concerned with principle, and determined not to endanger the national union. He insisted that Republicans accepted the constitutionality of slavery in the South, but that it was "an evil not to be extended." Furthermore, he asserted this was not a revolutionary principle but a conservative one based on the actions of the Founding Fathers when they organized the old "Northwest Territory," in which slavery was prohibited. Lincoln denounced southern condemnation of Republicans—"Black Republicans" they were called—saying Southerners exaggerated or ignored the party's position. He asked both sides to sit down and discuss the issue quietly and dispassionately. Similarly, he denounced such lawlessness as John Brown's raid.

Finally, Lincoln declared his certainty that the Republican position was a truly moral one

The rafters of the Wigwam, a hall built by the Republicans of Chicago to seat ten thousand convention delegates in 1860, shook with thunderous cheering when Lincoln won his party's presidential nomination on the third ballot. Supporters' confidence in Lincoln flowed largely from the preconvention speech he had made in New York. In that presentation he declared that the Republicans stood on the moral side of the slavery issue. His words were powerful and moving: "Let us have faith that right makes might, and in that faith, let us, to the end, dare to do our duty as we understand it."

The winning ticket: Lincoln and his running mate, Hannibal Hamlin of Maine (opposite), carried the support of farmers, laborers, and intellectuals to defeat the Democrats in the 1860 presidential race. Within six years of the founding of their party, the Republicans had displaced the Democrats as the dominant party in the Northeast and Middle West.

that would guarantee victory: "Let us have faith that right makes might, and in that faith, let us, to the end, dare to do our duty as we understand it." After this powerful speech, Lincoln was a force to be reckoned with in the Republican Party.

Meanwhile, the Democrats were busy tearing themselves apart. A nominating convention in Charleston broke up when Northerners and Southerners could not agree on a candidate. A second effort was made in Baltimore. There Douglas was nominated, but the Southerners refused to accept him and walked out. The bolters held still another convention and picked Vice President John Breckinridge as their candidate. The situation became even more confused when a group of moderates formed the Constitutional Union Party and nominated a former Whig, John Bell.

Although the Republicans were known primarily for their opposition to slavery, their campaign stressed other issues—corruption and blundering by the Democratic administra-

THE UNION MUST AND SHALL BE PRESERVED

FREE SPEECH.
FREE HOMES,
FREE TERRITORY.

PROTECTION TO AMERICAN INDUSTRY

FOR PRESIDENT
ABRAHAM LINCOLN
OF ILLINOIS

FOR VICE PRESIDENT
HANNIBAL HAMLIN
OF MAINE

tion, and the need for greater expenditures on internal improvements, a homestead measure, a higher tariff, and support of land-grant colleges. Lincoln himself made no speeches during the campaign. He did appear at a Republican rally in Springfield, Illinois; a report on this event was headed with a drawing of an elephant, one of the earliest known uses of what was to become the party symbol. Both Douglas and Bell campaigned on the overriding importance of maintaining the Union, while Breckinridge ran on a pro-slavery platform.

As might have been predicted, the result of the balloting was highly sectional. Breckinridge won the electoral votes of all the states of the Deep South, plus Maryland and Delaware, for a total of 72. Bell carried the border states of Kentucky, Tennessee, and Virginia, for 39 electoral votes. Douglas finished second in the popular vote, but won only in Missouri. (He also received three of New Jersey's seven electoral votes.)

Lincoln won virtually the entire North as well as California and Oregon for a total of 180 electoral votes. With more than half of the total of 303 electoral votes, Lincoln was elected. Still, he only received 40 percent of the popular vote. The question now was how would the South react? Would they believe the moderate position Lincoln had outlined at Cooper Union? Or would they succumb to the fears of "Black Republicanism" and make good their threat to leave the Union if Lincoln were elected?

The Civil War

Shortly after the election, and months before Lincoln's inauguration, America clearly faced a crisis. On December 20, 1860, South Carolina seceded from the Union. By the end of February 1861, six more southern states had followed suit. The seven states ignored compromise proposals and refused to wait and see what the new President would do. They followed the theory that, since they had voluntarily joined the Union, they were free to leave it at any time. South Carolina also presumed that all federal lands should be returned, and the state seized two federal military posts and an arsenal before the year was over.

President Buchanan denied the right of a state to secede, but he felt that the federal government had no right to forcibly oppose secession. He too fell back on attempts at compromise. The attempts were doomed to failure; Buchanan's policy simply meant that the problem was being left for Lincoln and the Republicans.

In February 1861, the seven states that had seceded formed the Confederate States of America, electing former U.S. Senator and Secretary of War Jefferson Davis as President. On March 4, Abraham Lincoln was inaugurated, and the Civil War broke out barely a month after that event, when Fort Sumter was attacked. The new President obviously had his work cut out for him.

Lincoln's inauguration was a crowded occasion, and peaceful, though the streets of Washington were lined with armed soldiers. The man who became President that day had the strength of character and courage necessary to face the great trial that was about to begin. Historians who have evaluated the careers of the American Presidents rank Lincoln only behind George Washington. Among those traits that enabled Lincoln to lead the United States through perhaps it most trying time were an even temper, extreme patience, honesty, diligence, humor, and, above all, commitment to principle.

Lincoln's inaugural address, though conciliatory, demonstrated that commitment to principle. He recognized the South's fear that "their property and their peace and personal security are endangered," but he denied there was "any reasonable cause" for their apprehension. Lincoln repeated an earlier statement: "I have no purpose, directly or indirectly, to interfere with the institution of slavery where it exists. I have no lawful right

to do so." But he stood firm in the face of the secession crisis, made no modification of his position against the extension of slavery, and warned that "the Union of these States is perpetual. . . . no State, upon its own mere motion, can lawfully get out of the Union. . . ."

Lincoln also made no concessions to the

As the Union's Commander-in-Chief, Lincoln visits officers of the Army of the Potomac encamped near Antietam Creek in Maryland. Disappointed that the troops had failed to pursue and destroy the retreating Army of Northern Virginia, thus shortening the war, Lincoln relieved George B. McClellan as commander of the federal army. Throughout the nation's bitterest struggle, Lincoln demonstrated magnanimity toward all factions to achieve his goal of national unity. During this time he masterfully rallied northern Democrats to the Union cause and molded the Republican Party into a strong national organization.

South in his appointment of Cabinet members. Rather, he unified the Republican Party by appointing his chief party rivals to key positions. William Seward, Salmon Chase, Simon Cameron, and Edward Bates became the Secretaries of State, Treasury, and War, and Attorney General respectively.

Careful as he was to avoid giving the South justification for secession, Lincoln clearly stated that he would not turn over southern forts to the states, and, if necessary, he would use force to preserve the Union. Lincoln thus served notice on the South without resorting to threats. The decisive moment was not long in coming. Fort Sumter, in South Carolina, was low on supplies, and Lincoln announced he was sending fresh provisions by sea. If the Confederate government allowed the fort to be resupplied, it would mean it was not serious about secession. But it was serious. On April 12, Confederate guns shelled the fort, starting four years of bloody fighting.

President Lincoln's reaction was immediate. Using his war powers, he issued a call for troops. All the northern governors responded promptly, and Democrat Stephen Douglas forgot past differences and pledged his support of the President. Just as the North rallied in this time of crisis, so did the South: Four more southern states seceded and joined the Confederacy. The four border states in which slavery was legal—Delaware, Maryland, Kentucky, and Missouri—remained loyal to the Union.

But not everyone in the North rallied to Lincoln's support. Opposition to Lincoln arose among different groups. Many Democrats refused to follow the lead of Douglas. "Peace Democrats," often called by the derogatory name "Copperheads," did not support the war, and held that the South should be allowed to leave the Union peacefully. Then in June 1861, Douglas' death deprived Lincoln of his foremost Democratic supporter.

Even among the Republicans there was a great difference of opinion. One faction, which has become known as the Radical Republicans, wanted a drastic change in policy.

Lincoln and his congressional followers insisted that the war was being fought to preserve the Union. The Radicals, under the leadership of Representative Thaddeus Stevens and Senators Charles Sumner and Benjamin Wade, were determined to turn the war's purpose from preservation of the Union to the abolition of slavery.

Lincoln balked at this idea. He preferred to restore the Union as it had been, while planning the gradual elimination of slavery. Besides believing this was the proper course, Lincoln feared that introduction of the abolition question would divide the North. Indeed, he was right; later in the war there were draft riots by those opposed to fighting over slavery. Lincoln also knew the Union still included four slave states, and that their continued support was important to the war effort.

Lincoln and his Radical Republican critics were equally sure they were right. The quarrel continued for a year and a half, but publicly Lincoln would not budge. In a famous letter he wrote to answer the criticisms of editor Horace Greeley, Lincoln—despite having already prepared an emancipation proclamation—repeated both his personal hatred for slavery and his presidential duty of restoring the Union: "My paramount object in this struggle *is* to save the Union, and is *not* either to save or to destroy slavery. If I could save the Union without freeing *any* slave I would do it, and if I could save it by freeing *all* the slaves I would do it; and if I could save it by freeing some and leaving others alone I would also do that. . . . I have here stated my purpose according to my view of *official* duty; and I intend no modification of my oft-expressed *personal* wish that all men every where could be free."

Lincoln no doubt looked forward to the day when his personal belief in universal freedom and his presidential responsibilities to preserve the Union coincided. Actually, slow progress was being made toward making an end to slavery a key objective of the war. In May 1861, Union general Benjamin Butler had declared captured slaves "contraband of

war," and therefore subject to confiscation—which meant freedom. Three months later Congress passed, and Lincoln signed, a Confiscation Act. This act declared that any slave who worked on Confederate fortifications would be confiscated. The following March, Lincoln recommended a program of compensated emancipation to the four loyal slave states, though they rejected the idea. A month later, slavery was abolished in the District of Columbia, and in June, in all the territories.

Meanwhile, the fighting was going badly for the North. Lincoln could not find a satisfactory commander, and the South suffered no serious setback. Between August 9 and September 15, 1862, the North was defeated in three major battles. Lincoln must have been frustrated. He had already decided to issue a "bombshell" announcement, but was waiting for a victory so it would not seem to be a step

A democracy has no room for master or slave maintained Lincoln, seated at the reading of the first draft of his Emancipation Proclamation. To the left are Secretary of War Stanton and Secretary of the Treasury Chase; to the right, Secretary of the Navy Welles, Secretary of State Seward, Secretary of the Interior Smith, Postmaster General Blair, and Attorney General Bates. The immortal proclamation, issued on New Year's Day of 1863, declared that all slaves within the Confederacy were forever free.

taken in desperation. His opportunity came when a Confederate invasion of the North was halted in the bloody Battle of Antietam, on September 17. The President wasted no time. Five days later, he issued the preliminary Emancipation Proclamation.

The Emancipation Proclamation is a prime example of carrot-and-stick diplomacy. President Lincoln's "carrot" was clear: If, during the following one hundred days, the Southerners laid down their arms and returned to the Union, there would be no attempt to disturb their "peculiar institution." But if they continued in rebellion, the stick would be used: Slaves in any state still in revolt would be declared "forever free," and their freedom would be protected by the federal government. Since the seceding states refused to accept the carrot, the stick was applied. On January 1, 1863, all slaves in the rebel states were declared free.

Two important aspects of the Emancipation Proclamation must be kept in mind. First, it was designed as a war measure, to injure the South's capacity to continue fighting. Therefore, it did not apply in the loyal border states. Second, it had little immediate effect, since the areas to which it applied were in the hands of the Confederates, and they ignored it. But as Union troops occupied more southern territory, slaves escaped to their lines and claimed the freedom the underground grapevine had informed them about—and emancipation became a reality. Not until the 13th Amendment was ratified in 1865 was slavery finally abolished as an institution.

Lincoln's timing was flawless. Had he followed the wishes of the Radical Republicans and declared emancipation earlier, most Northerners probably would have rejected him and turned against the war. But Lincoln understood the people, and he waited until public opinion had come around to this position. Still, the first elections following the Emancipation Proclamation went badly for the Republicans. Democrats won six northern states and almost doubled their representation in the House of Representatives. Lincoln had

held the reigns on the impatient until the North was prepared to see the war through, even if saving the Union had not remained the war's sole purpose.

Reconstruction

Even issuance of the Emancipation Proclamation was not enough to satisfy the President's Republican opponents. Lincoln and the Radicals simply moved on to a new battleground—Reconstruction. The two sides differed on vir-

According to Lincoln, the South may have separated itself from its proper relationship to the other states, but it had never officially left the Union. The Radicals, on the other hand, believed that, illegal or not, secession was a fact. Senator Charles Sumner compared the southern action to "state suicide," while Representative Thaddeus Stevens claimed the seceding areas could be treated as "conquered provinces," with none of the rights of states.

President Lincoln felt the presidential power to grant pardons gave him the power to

A cow on a grassy sod roof drew scant notice from homesteaders, such as this Nebraska family which fashioned its house from a hillside. Despite the pall cast by the Civil War, the Republican administration compiled an impressive record of national legislation. One long-awaited bill, the Homestead Act, became law in 1862. It provided for inexpensive land in western states, thus encouraging settlers to follow Horace Greeley's adage: "Go West, young man."

control Reconstruction. Congress, however, insisted on its power in the process by virtue of its right to pass on admission of states to House and Senate representation. The first clash ended in stalemate. In December 1863, Lincoln declared that if 10 percent of the 1860 voters in any southern state took an oath of loyalty to the Union—and the state agreed to emancipation—the state's government would be recognized. Arkansas and Louisiana accepted Lincoln's formula in 1864, but the Radicals refused to seat members sent to Congress from those states.

Congress took the next step, in the form of the Wade-Davis Bill. Under this legislation, a majority of a southern state's electorate would have to pledge loyalty to the Union, slavery would have to be abolished, and Confederate military and civil leaders disenfranchised before the state would be allowed to return. Lincoln believed such harsh measures would produce lingering bitterness, so he pocket-vetoed the bill. The stalemate continued.

In 1864, even in the midst of a bloody war, the nation prepared for a presidential election. To overcome political bickering, Lincoln encouraged pro-war Democrats to join Republicans in a "Union Party." The coalition served a dual purpose. First, it made it clear to the American people that the war was not a partisan battle, broadening popular support for Lincoln's policies. Second, it helped to reduce the power of the Radicals by providing a conservative counterweight. The Radicals were preempted by Lincoln's policies, and the President had little difficulty in gaining renomination at the 1864 National Union Convention. In addition, Lincoln was able to persuade the convention to choose a border state pro-war Democrat, Tennessee's Andrew Johnson, as the vice presidential candidate. The party platform promised to continue the war until successful and to end slavery through constitutional amendment.

The Democrats nominated Gen. George McClellan, whose lack of military success had forced Lincoln to fire him. McClellan was a pro-war Democrat, but his party's platform declared the war effort a failure and called for restoration of the Union as it had been—meaning, with slavery still protected in the South. Many people in both parties expected a Democratic victory, but the North won a series of battles in the months before the election and Lincoln ended up with about 55 percent of the popular vote and a 212 to 21 vote victory in the electoral college.

Lincoln's second inaugural address was one of the greatest speeches in history. The brilliance of Gen. Ulysses S. Grant's military strategy had already brought the South to the edge of defeat. President Lincoln realized this, and he looked forward to the need to reunify the American people. He was prepared to extend the hand of friendship to the South. He knew many Southerners had opposed disunion—and were eager to return to their traditional loyalty—if the North was not vindictive. Then, on April 9, 1865, at Virginia's Appomatox Court House, Gen. Robert E. Lee surrendered the last major southern army to Grant, and the war was almost over.

A few nights later, President Lincoln made the fateful decision to attend a play at Ford's Theatre, where he was shot by John Wilkes Booth. Lincoln died just one month after beginning his second term as President, and, in accordance with the Constitution, Andrew Johnson became President. Johnson meant to follow the program begun by Lincoln, but he lacked the ability, the personality, and the political support needed in those difficult days. Moreover, he was a former slave owner who showed little concern for the welfare of the free blacks. His problems began almost as soon as he took office.

While Congress was away on summer recess, Johnson began putting into effect a Reconstruction program that was neither as lenient as Lincoln had wanted nor as harsh as demanded by the Wade-Davis Bill. He recognized the governments that had been created by Lincoln in Arkansas, Louisiana, and Tennessee. He offered pardons to those who promised future loyalty, except for Confederate leaders. Johnson set no percentage of loy-

On March 30, 1867—two years after the
assassination of Lincoln—Secretary of State
William H. Seward (seated at left) and Russia's
minister to the U.S., Baron Edoard de Stoeckl
(standing at globe), consummate the purchase of
Alaska. Seward had convinced the Russians to sell
the vast northern wilderness for less than two
cents an acre. For years known as "Seward's
Folly," Alaska (which later joined the Union as
the 49th state) turned out to be a bargain rich in
fish, furs, minerals, and timber.

alty oaths necessary for a state to be considered reconstructed, but he left the strong impression that he demanded a majority. Furthermore, each southern government had to repeal the ordinance of secession, abolish slavery, and repudiate the war debt.

By the time Congress met in December 1865, the southern states had fulfilled Johnson's requirements, with a few exceptions. But many Northerners did not believe Southerners' actions conformed to their words. Black Codes passed by southern legislatures severely limited the rights of the freed slaves; there were a series of race riots in which many blacks were killed; and some of the representatives sent to Congress had been leading secessionists—including Confederate Vice President Alexander Stephens. Because of this, Congress rejected Johnson's program.

One of the first acts of the Radical-controlled Congress was to deny seats to the representatives sent from the southern states.

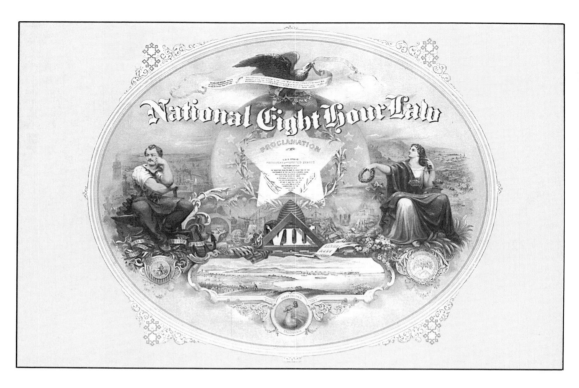

Instead, the Radicals created the Committee on Reconstruction to investigate conditions in the South and recommend a policy. The Radicals also passed a civil rights act—over the President's veto—forbidding states from discriminating on the basis of race. They were undoubtedly idealistic as well as radical, and they followed up their first victory by adopting the 14th Amendment. Under its provisions, blacks were recognized as citizens. Also, persons who had taken an oath to support the Constitution but had then joined the Confederacy were disqualified from holding office until Congress forgave them. Each southern state had to ratify this amendment before it would be readmitted to the Union.

Following an overwhelming victory in the congressional elections of 1866, the Radicals devised the final plan for Reconstruction. It took the form of three acts, each of which was passed over President Johnson's veto. Military governments were given control of the South, whites were not allowed to register to vote without taking a loyalty oath that satisfied the registrar, and blacks were encouraged to become voters. This led to the 15th Amendment, giving blacks the right to vote everywhere in the Union.

Distressed by Johnson's refusal to adopt a harsh scheme of Reconstruction, and by his open opposition to their program, the Radicals sought to impeach the President. Their excuse for action was Johnson's violation of the Tenure of Office Act. Passed in 1867, the law denied the President the right to remove civil officials without the consent of the Senate. President Johnson believed the Tenure of Office Act was unconstitutional, and he was willing to test it in court. He dismissed Secretary of War Edwin Stanton, a man who had worked with the Radicals against Johnson.

According to the Radicals, Johnson's action fit the grounds for impeachment outlined in the Constitution: high crimes or misdemeanors. The House voted to impeach the President and presented 11 charges against him to the Senate for trial. Though the trial was obviously caused by political disagreements rather than by any "crime," it created one of the most dramatic scenes in American history. Tremendous political pressure was placed on all Republican senators to vote for Johnson's impeachment. But seven Republicans—including Edmund Ross of Kansas, who was immortalized in John F. Kennedy's *Profiles in Courage*, and John Grimes of Iowa, who was carried in on a stretcher—refused to go along, and the first three charges lost by a single vote. At that point the Radicals gave up and dropped the remaining charges.

Defeat in the impeachment effort did not prevent the Radicals from imposing their harsh Reconstruction policy on the South. Spurring them on was the rise of strong southern opposition to military rule and to the state governments that had been formed. These governments, to the dismay of most white Southerners, were controlled by a coalition of former slaves, Northerners who had come to the South with the Union armies or afterwards ("carpetbaggers"), and Southerners who supported them ("scalawags"). One reaction was widespread violence and intimidation of blacks and Radical Republican sympathizers. Secret societies, including the notorious Ku Klux Klan, were mostly to blame for the violence.

While the Senate considered impeaching Andrew Johnson and the South fought Reconstruction, the Republican National Convention met to nominate candidates for the 1868 presidential race. With near unanimity, the party chose the great hero of the Civil War, Gen. Ulysses S. Grant. His political positions were virtually unknown, but he was honest, widely respected, and had cooperated with the Republican leadership in the dispute over the firing of Secretary Stanton. The platform praised the congressional Reconstruction policy, but, because of differences within the party, avoided strong stands on other issues. Horatio Seymour, Governor of New York, provided the Democratic opposition.

Even though Republicans had repudiated their own administration, they were in a strong position. The party had led the country

Civil War hero Gen. Ulysses S. Grant won the Republican presidential nomination by acclamation in 1868. The American people, weary of turmoil and hoping for reform, expected Grant to bring the same brilliance and vigor to the Presidency that he had displayed in a series of inspiring Union victories that ended the War Between the States. But during his two terms in office, Grant seemed bewildered by his role as Chief Executive. He delegated major responsibilities to subordinates. They took advantage of his honesty and trust, and his administration was rocked by scandals, followed by financial panic.

Relief for overworked federal employees: In 1868— near the end of Andrew Johnson's Presidency— Congress passed the National Eight Hour Law, depicted by the lithograph opposite. The bill, which prescribed the length of a workday, applied only to government workers. Four years later, Congress set a precedent when it authorized equal pay for equal work performed by women employed by federal agencies.

through a terrible war, and that was not its only success. In foreign policy, strong support of the Monroe Doctrine persuaded France to withdraw its troops from Mexico, allowing the Mexican people to overthrow the puppet government of Maximilian and Carlotta. And Russia was removed from North America when Secretary of State Seward negotiated the purchase of Alaska.

At home there were also great advances. The Republicans could claim credit for many popular legislative enactments. The Homestead Act of 1862 gave land-hungry settlers the opportunity to obtain public lands in the West simply by living on and cultivating their claims for five years. The same year Congress passed the Land-Grant Act, sponsored by Republican leader Justin Morrill. Under its terms, land was given to the states, and the proceeds from the sale of that land were set aside to be used for education. It was the basis for the land-grant colleges that have been a key part of the American educational system for more than one hundred years.

Higher tariffs favored by Republican legislators gave a big boost to industrial development, and, immediately after the war, construction began on the first transcontinental railroad. The country was at peace, it was generally prosperous, and the outcome of the 1868 election was never really in doubt. Though the popular vote was fairly close, Grant defeated Seymour easily in the electoral college, 214 to 80.

Grant's years as President can only be termed unfortunate. His background had not prepared him for the office, and he turned out to be both an inadequate administrator and a poor judge of character. Nevertheless, his first term was not unsuccessful. The Radical Republicans supervised the Reconstruction of the last of the seceding states. Grant created the first Civil Service Commission, though no real reform was yet enacted. By supporting "greenbacks" he was able to defuse the growing discontent of indebted farmers. And, through the careful diplomacy of Grant's talented Secretary of State, Hamilton Fish, a

treaty was signed with England, ending years of dispute involving claims on both sides and ushering in an era of better relations with Canada as well as with England.

But troubles also arose during Grant's first term. The Republicans lost a large number of seats in the congressional elections of 1870.

East and West shake hands after crews laid the last section of track for the first transcontinental railroad. To link the Midwest with the Pacific coast, the Union Pacific crews (on the right) worked westward from Omaha, Nebraska. The Central Pacific gang (on the left) pushed the railhead eastward from Sacramento, California. The two lines merged at Promontory Point, Utah, on May 10, 1869. In less than six years the rival railroads had laid track across the nation's highest range of mountains and through its bleakest basins. During the course of the epic venture, the construction gangs of the Central Pacific laid as much as ten miles of rails a day—a record that remains unsurpassed.

And there was growing division within the party itself. Senator Carl Schurz led opponents of the Grant Administration in forming a Liberal Republican movement, which stood for lower tariffs, civil service reform, and amnesty for disenfranchised Confederates. The liberals nominated old reformer Horace Greeley for President in 1872, and he was then picked by the Democrats as well. Still, Grant was easily reelected, with increased margins in both the popular vote and the electoral college.

Grant's joy at his success was short-lived. A financial panic, the result of both national and international economic problems, struck the country. In 1874, Democrats regained control of the House and cut the Republican margin in the Senate. Then a devastating series of scandals struck the administration. Grant's personal honesty was never questioned, but the country and the Republican Party were rocked by the revelations.

The Gilded Age

Historians give names to specific periods in order to make them easier to understand. The last quarter of the 19th century is called the Gilded Age. It is not a flattering description. Something gilded may look valuable but may be worthless underneath. In the context of this period the name refers to the government corruption too often just beneath the surface at the local, state, and national levels. Certainly there was corruption in this period, but more important, this was a time of great national advancements. Just as the Republicans can be blamed for some of the corruption that existed, they must also be credited with leading many of the advances.

The Reconstruction of the South ended in the midst of great controversy surrounding the presidential election of 1876. Republicans found themselves divided again. The "Stalwarts" wanted to nominate Grant for a third term, but the "Half-Breeds" opposed this. They wanted a candidate who was not associated with the scandals of the day, a man who could gain the support of Schurz and the Liberal Republicans. It took seven ballots before the national convention finally decided on Rutherford B. Hayes. It was a good choice. Hayes had been a Union general, was the successful three-term governor of Ohio, and was known to support civil service reform. The Democrats also picked a good man, New York Governor Samuel J. Tilden, who had become famous for prosecuting the corrupt Tammany Hall organization of his own party.

Both candidates spoke out for civil service reform and for the withdrawal of troops from the South, and they held similar views on the economic issues of the day. The result of the campaign was the closest election in American history. Tilden received a tiny majority of the popular vote, but there was no agreement in the electoral college. Tilden led 184 to 165, with 185 necessary for the election; the votes of three states were in dispute because of reported irregularities. Congress created an electoral commission to determine who would receive the 20 disputed votes. The commission eventually awarded all the votes to Hayes, and he became President by a one-vote margin.

Democrats were bitter at the election results and refused to cooperate with Hayes. Since they had a majority in the House of Representatives, there was a stalemate in the government, and Hayes was unable to accomplish as much as was expected of him. In spite of this, his administration was by no means a failure. He kept his campaign promise to withdraw federal troops from the South, helping decrease the bitterness many Southerners still felt. Hayes helped advance the cause of a merit system in the civil service by appointing Carl Schurz Secretary of the Interior and supporting his refusal to allow patronage appointments. The President also signed an act designed to remove some of the legal inequalities suffered by women, helping Belva Ann Bennett Lockwood become the first woman declared eligible for admittance to practice before the U.S. Supreme Court.

Republican symbol, the elephant trumpets in triumph at the defeat of the Democrats in the elections of 1875. The victory assured the reform of New York's Tammany Hall, the renowned stronghold of the powerful Democratic political boss William Marcy Tweed. His infamous "Tweed Ring" had plundered vast sums of the taxpayer's money from the New York City treasury. The work of political cartoonist Thomas Nast in Harper's Weekly *exposed Tweed and led to his arrest. The first known use of the Republican Party's symbol occurred in 1860 when the* Illinois State Journal *put an elephant at the head of its report on a speech given by presidential candidate Abraham Lincoln. It was Nast's cartoons, however, that firmly established the elephant and the donkey as the symbols of the Republican and Democratic Parties.*

Rutherford B. Hayes brought dignity, honesty, and modest reform to the White House. A one-electoral-vote margin in 1877 gave him the Presidency in the most bitterly disputed election in American history. Though a Democratic-controlled House of Representatives blocked many programs proposed by Hayes, he still pushed through some accomplishments. They included the withdrawal of federal troops from the South and the advancement of a sound merit system in the civil service. Hayes also signed an act designed to reduce legal inequities suffered by women. The new law helped Belva Ann Bennett Lockwood to become the first woman eligible for admittance to practice before the Supreme Court.

A Republican campaign poster for the presidential race in 1880 (opposite) portrays James A. Garfield and his running mate, Chester A. Arthur. President for only six months, Garfield died from an assassin's bullet. An embittered attorney who had been denied a consular post stepped up to President Garfield in a Washington, D.C., railroad station and fired the fatal shot.

But few politicians seemed terribly upset when President Hayes declared he would not seek reelection. Hayes' decision to retire led to another struggle between Stalwarts and Half-Breeds. At the 1880 Republican convention, 36 ballots were needed to nominate a compromise candidate. The man chosen was a moderate Half-Breed, James A. Garfield. To balance the ticket and console the losing faction, a Stalwart, Chester A. Arthur, was picked to be Garfield's running mate. In a campaign that was not distinguished by concentration on the issues, Garfield won a close but clearcut victory over Democrat Winfield Scott Hancock, and the Republicans carried narrow majorities in both the House and Senate.

After only a few months in office, President Garfield was assassinated by a crazed office seeker disappointed by his failure to receive a patronage appointment. Garfield's death elevated Arthur to the Presidency. Reform-minded Republicans were upset because Arthur was known as a spoilsman, a man whose political advance had been due largely to patronage appointments. As so often is the case, however, the man grew into the office, and the high quality of Arthur's Presidency was a pleasant surprise to many.

During his term in office, President Arthur sponsored a bill that brought about the rebirth of the American Navy. Very little had been spent on the Navy since the Civil War, and by the 1880s American naval power was negligible. But there was increasing belief that sea power was the key to a strong and independent nation, and Arthur took advantage of this feeling. He also had the courage to veto a pork-barrel rivers and harbors bill. Arthur's most important accomplishment, however, was the Pendleton Act, passed in 1883.

Much of the credit for the Pendleton Act must go to James Garfield. His murder outraged the American people. When it was learned he had been killed by a frustrated spoils seeker, there was an insistent demand for civil service reform. Arthur took advantage of the popular mood—and of the fact that both parties' most recent platforms had given

OUR NATION'S CHOICE.

HARMONY, PEACE AND PROSPERITY.

OUR COUNTRY FOREVER

OUR NATION'S HONOR WILL BE PRESERVED.

Gen. JAMES ABRAM GARFIELD,
Republican Candidate for President.

Gen. CHESTER A. ARTHUR,
Republican Candidate for Vice-President.

THE PLATFORM OF THE **REPUBLICAN PARTY,** ADOPTED AT THE Convention in Chicago, JUNE 28, 1880.

DEVOTION TO THE UNION.

Raised to the Presidency by the death of Garfield, Chester A. Arthur championed civil service reform, to the dismay of old friends who advocated the return of the spoils system. During Arthur's administration, Congress passed the Pendleton Act. The measure set up a bipartisan Civil Service Commission, established competitive written examinations for certain government positions, and protected employees against removal from their jobs for political reasons.

lip service to the issue—by pressing Congress to pass the Pendleton Act. The act created a bipartisan three-man Civil Service Commission, entrusted with determining on a merit basis the fitness of federal appointees. The act included a ban on nepotism and on fund solicitation from officeholders; it created a list of jobs that could only be filled on the basis of competitive examinations; and it set a probation period for new jobholders. From that time on, the United States has had an increasingly professional civil service.

Despite these important achievements, Arthur was not a popular figure, and he was denied the presidential nomination in 1884. By that time the Republican Party was firmly in the hands of the Half-Breed faction, and that group insisted that the nomination go to its longtime leader, James G. Blaine. Though he was to lose the presidential election, Blaine was an important figure in the years between Lincoln and Theodore Roosevelt. He spent 18 years as a member of Congress, serving in both House and Senate, and he was Speaker of the House for six years. Later, he spent almost four years as Secretary of State and was primarily responsible for organizing the Pan-American Congress and for negotiating tariff reciprocity treaties—both of which greatly improved the image of the United States in Central and South America. Blaine also began two efforts that were not successful for many years, but which illustrate his farsightedness. One was to build a canal across the Isthmus of Panama, and the other was to put an end to the unrestrained killing of fur seals.

Unfortunately for Blaine, people as prominent in public life for as long as he was often make almost as many enemies as friends. This may explain why he won the presidential nomination only once. He ran against Grover Cleveland in what probably was the most shameful campaign in American history, although the standards of the two candidates were higher than that of their followers. Religious slurs and accusations of political and personal immorality took the place of issues. Complicating matters, former Democrat and

Republican Benjamin Butler ran for President on the Greenback Party ticket, and another Republican ran as the candidate of the Prohibition Party.

Blaine appeared to have a lead late in the campaign, but a careless remark by one of his supporters referring to the Democratic opposition as the party of "Rum, Romanism, and Rebellion"—and Blaine's failure to disavow the remark—cost him the votes of many Catholics, the electoral vote of New York, and probably the election itself. It was a very close race, and neither Blaine nor Cleveland won a popular majority, but Cleveland eked out a 219-182 margin in the electoral college. The Democrats also won a majority in the House, but the Republicans controlled the Senate.

This division of power was extremely important, for two reasons. First, the tariff was the most important issue of the day, and, unlike the Republicans, Cleveland believed in a very low tariff. However, the Republican Senate, and sometimes even the House, where many Democrats also believed in a protective tariff, was able to prevent a major change in American policy. Second, there was a shift in the center of power, as Congress eclipsed the President in the last quarter of the 19th century.

The House boasted such strong and talented leaders as Republican Speakers J. Warren Keifer and the witty master of House rules, Thomas B. Reed. And there was the young congressman who steered the important tariff bill of 1890 through the House, William McKinley.

Even so, the House was outshone by the Senate. Justin Morrill, father of the land-grant colleges, remained in the Upper House until his death in 1898. John Sherman, brother of Civil War hero William T. Sherman, was principal author of two of the most important pieces of legislation of the era—the Silver Purchase Act, which defused rising farm unrest, and the Antitrust Act, which helped prevent the growth of monopolies.

The great master of tariff law for many years was Nelson Aldrich (grandfather of

Disappointed standard bearer, James G. Blaine lost a close presidential race to Grover Cleveland in 1884; it was the first Republican defeat for the land's highest office in 24 years. Nevertheless, Blaine served his party with distinction for nearly 40 years. He was a congressman, a senator, Speaker of the House for six years, Secretary of State for nearly four years. He helped improve the image of the United States in Central and South America by promoting the creation of the Pan-American Congress and by negotiating tariff reciprocity treaties. Two goals that he worked toward without success demonstrated his farsightedness: a canal across the Isthmus of Panama and a ban on the unrestricted killing of fur seals.

Calling for a protective tariff, a campaign illustration highlights a controversial issue in the 1888 presidential contest. The election ended in victory for Benjamin Harrison and a Republican sweep of the House and the Senate. Significant legislation during Harrison's term included a high-tariff bill, silver purchase bills, and the Sherman Antitrust Act—the first federal measure attempting to protect trade and commerce against unlawful restraints and monopolies.

Nelson A. Rockefeller). In addition, there were the men who ran the Senate for a generation—Orville Platt, William Allison, Mark Hanna, Boies Penrose, and Matt Quay—Republicans all. Under Republican and Democratic administrations alike, these were the men who kept the government running smoothly.

Following the Republicans' only loss in a presidential race since Frémont's failure in 1856, a unified convention met in 1888, determined to drive Grover Cleveland from the White House. The contest for the nomination was a free-for-all. Blaine wanted a second chance, but could not arouse much support. The strength of the Senate's Republican contingent was seen in the fact that all of the leading presidential candidates were senators: John Sherman, William B. Allison, and Benjamin Harrison. Harrison slowly overcame Sherman's early lead, and the grandson of

President William Henry Harrison was nominated on the eighth ballot.

The race of 1888 was another in the series of close elections in the Gilded Age. Harrison won narrowly, with a count of 238 to 168 electoral votes, even though Cleveland received about 100,000 more popular votes. The Republican Party also won control of both Houses of Congress, and it was these Republican majorities that passed the important tariff, antitrust, and silver purchase bills of 1890. Six new states were added to the Union in 1889-90, and the congressmen from those states added much to the strength of progressive Republicanism. This advantage was balanced by cool relations between the President and Congress, largely due to Harrison's aloof personality.

Eastern opposition to the tariff of 1890, along with a rising western and southern demand for inflationary policies that most Republicans could not accept, led to a drastic defeat in the congressional elections of 1890. Discontented farmers formed the Populist Party, winning a number of congressional seats in traditional Republican strongholds. In other races they took enough votes to allow Democrats to win. Though the Republicans were able to retain a majority in the Senate, the Democrats gained a large margin in the House.

Divided power in Congress again resulted in political stalemate. Little of importance was accomplished, and both parties looked forward to the 1892 elections. These elections were a rerun of 1888—Harrison against Cleveland, with the tariff as the major issue dividing the parties. But times were different. The economy had taken a downward turn, and labor unrest had spread through much of the country. These conditions encouraged the Populists to run their own candidate, James Weaver. Weaver cut deeply into Republican strength, gathering more than one million ballots and winning 22 electoral votes in the West.

It was in the East that the election was decided, however, and it was there that Cleveland won, becoming the only President to serve two noncontinuous terms. Cleveland received only 3 percent more votes than Harrison, but won 277-145 in the electoral college. Also, the Democrats won majorities in both Senate and House. For the first time since the Civil War, the Republican Party was shut out.

The Republican Revival

The setback of 1892 forced the Republican Party to reexamine itself. Originally it had been a sectional party, representing the majority in the most populous area of the country. As more and more western territories became states, the party sought to broaden its appeal, and with some success. But the heart of Republican strength remained in the small towns and rural areas of the North and the Midwest. The party's policies, particularly the high tariff and support for business, reflected the attitudes of the people in those areas.

Now, however, the traditional Republican territory contained a shrinking portion of the electorate. In the growing western states, farmers and miners demanded inflationary policies that were contrary to the best interests of eastern Republicans. Even more important, rising immigration and urbanization were shifting power in the East to big city political machines, most of which were in the hands of the Democrats.

As Republicans tried to regroup and fashion policies that would forge their national majority, economic collapse made their task easier than it might have been. The panic of 1893 began a four-year depression, the worst America had experienced up to that time. Depression in Europe, increasing competition around the world for American farm products, overexpansion by American industry, and a gold shortage were the major causes of the panic. But, as usual, most people blamed the party in power. Not surprisingly, the congressional elections of 1894 resulted in a tremendous Republican comeback, with the party regaining control of both Houses of

Wealthy and powerful Cleveland businessman and chairman of the Republican National Committee, Marcus Alonzo Hanna secured large contributions from eastern Republicans to help ensure the presidential nomination for his friend William McKinley. The return of prosperity to the nation in the late 1890s accounted greatly for the immense popularity that McKinley enjoyed as President. The national sense of well-being also gave added luster to the newly coined label, Grand Old Party.

Rolling up his sleeves, William McKinley (opposite) considers the advantages of digging a canal across the Isthmus of Panama, a shorter route than the one proposed across Nicaragua. A bustling nation on its way to becoming a world power inspired this cartoon in 1899. Following the nation's 1898 victory over Spain in a 100-day war, imperialist sentiment grew throughout the United States. Under McKinley, the nation acquired its first overseas possessions: the Philippines, Guam, and Puerto Rico.

Congress. Republican-Populist coalition candidates even won a number of supposedly solid Democratic seats in the South.

The Democrats, less unified than the Republicans, weakened themselves with party squabbling. In his campaign, President Cleveland had promised to lower the tariff considerably, but high-tariff Democrats in the Senate combined with Republicans to prevent this, and Cleveland angered many in his party when he bowed to the Senate's wishes. The President upset the public by refusing to support inflationary monetary policies and by turning to banker J.P. Morgan for aid in fighting the depression. As a result, Cleveland was accused of being a tool of Wall Street.

All the signs were good for the Republican Party as the 1896 presidential election approached. Depression and the Democratic divisions made the Republican nomination an eagerly sought prize. But it was not much of a contest. Ohio's William McKinley was one of the party's most popular figures, and he had the untiring support of a talented and powerful figure in both the party and the business community: Marcus Alonzo Hanna. McKinley easily turned back the challenge of House Speaker Thomas Reed, though Reed was backed by such rising Republican stars as Theodore Roosevelt and Henry Cabot Lodge. Reed had no chance. Given his widespread connections in both business and politics, Mark Hanna engineered McKinley's nomination on the first ballot.

The Democrats not only turned away from Cleveland, they also repudiated the conservative ideas he represented. To oppose McKinley, they chose the hero of the inflationary western wing of the party, William Jennings Bryan. Both parties suffered internal splits. Democrats who refused to support the platform promise of the free coinage of silver bolted their party; conversely Republicans who wanted free coinage left their own party. At the start of the campaign, the Populist Party provided a third choice. But the Populists joined the Democrats, since Bryan was a hero to many of them, too, and the Demo-

cratic platform adopted Populist ideas on silver, the tariff, and other major issues.

After a spirited campaign, McKinley won by the largest popular vote margin since 1872 and a convincing 271-176 spread in the electoral college. With the aid of strong Senate leadership and Speaker Reed's firm control of the House, McKinley's administration was quite successful. The return of prosperity coincided with the beginning of McKinley's term. The President and his party both hit new peaks of popularity, a popularity captured in the newly coined Republican label, Grand Old Party. Prosperity ended demands for inflationary policies, and industrial expansion, aided by a slightly increased tariff, was well on the way to making the United States the world's greatest industrial power.

But even prosperity took a backseat to the era's great headline-grabbing event, the war with Spain. Imperialism was a rising force in the United States during the last years of the 19th century, and the explosion that blew up the battleship *Maine* (to this day, no one knows what caused it) provided a great excuse to join the rush for colonies by taking over those controlled by Spain. Despite wartime enthusiasms, the American people and their leadership preferred to believe that American policy was humanitarian and democratic. An amendment attached to the Declaration of War against Spain denied the United States' intention of annexing Cuba and promised that island its independence. After its military victory, the United States bought the Philippines from Spain as part of the peace treaty and was ceded Puerto Rico. Both countries were quickly granted civilian governments, though half a century would pass before either nation gained its independence.

A second foreign affairs success resulted from the diplomacy of McKinley's Secretary of

"You may fire when you are ready, Gridley." Thus Commodore George Dewey (on the platform high above a gun mount of the Olympic) *launched the decisive battle of Manila Bay at 5:40 a.m. on May 1, 1898. For seven hours Dewey's outnumbered squadron of four cruisers and two gunboats raked the Spanish line from end to end. By early afternoon the ten vessels of the Spanish fleet were destroyed, silenced, or captured. No American ships suffered damage. The battle took the lives of 381 Spanish. U.S. casualties: eight wounded. Dewey's victory in the Philippines brought resistance in the Pacific theater of the Spanish-American War to a quick end. It also signaled the beginning of the U.S. as a major Asiatic power with political interests in Far Eastern affairs.*

State, John Hay. At this time, China was controlled by European powers, and both American business interests and missionaries were concerned they would not be allowed to continue their activity in that country. Secretary Hay agreed with them, and also felt that America should be treated as an equal of the European nations. He announced that the United States believed in an "open door" policy. This policy held that China should remain independent and that all nations should have equal rights to trade with her. None of the European nations officially accepted the policy, but none wished to argue the point, and it was abided by.

The Republican successes meant that the party did not suffer the normal off-year losses in the elections of 1898. Besides holding their own in the congressional races, the Republicans had a new hero arise on the national scene. The man who gained fame for leading troops up Cuba's San Juan Hill was elected governor of New York: Theodore Roosevelt.

Roosevelt was not a favorite of Republican regulars because of his independence, but he had great personal popularity. When it came time to choose nominees for the election of 1900, there was no doubt McKinley was the man. But his Vice President, Garret A. Hobart, had died. The perfect replacement seemed to be Governor Roosevelt. He would strengthen the ticket both in New York and in the West, where he was respected for his active and courageous life-style. And he would be "out of the hair" of the New York political leaders with whom he could not get along. Though Roosevelt wasn't happy about a nomination to what was considered a political graveyard, he could not turn down the convention delegates' unanimous vote.

McKinley and Roosevelt easily defeated the 1900 Democratic nominee, again William Jennings Bryan. Outside of the Democratic "Solid South," the Republicans only lost four states, and they retained firm control of Congress. McKinley did not have long to enjoy the victory, however. In September 1901 he attended the Pan-American Exposition at Buffalo, New York, to deliver a major speech calling for trade reciprocity. Tragically, the significance of the speech was blown away by a madman's bullet. Barely six months after his second inauguration, McKinley became the third Republican President in 36 years to die at the hands of an assassin.

Theodore Roosevelt

Although most of our Presidents have been men of talent and ability, Theodore Roosevelt was unique. His background seemed to embody the American experience. Roosevelt was born, raised, and educated in the East, but he went to the West and experienced frontier life firsthand. He wrote history books and led troops in Cuba. He was equally at home amidst crowds of potential voters and in private audiences with popes and kings. He could demand political reforms and still cooperate with less than saintly political leaders. His wide range of interests, his energy, and his talent gained him the respect of a wide spectrum of the American people. He was, in the words of historian Earl Schenck Miers, "the flower of progressivism, who dined with a Negro, put a Jew in his Cabinet, and muckraked the muckrakers."

Roosevelt's early political career had been most unusual. In fact, his choice of a career was unusual. Well-bred young men of his day were not expected to lower themselves to a lifetime in politics. He was probably drawn to public service by the desire to clean up corruption. He stayed because he was intrigued by the power available to the successful politician. Running as a reformer, Roosevelt was first elected to the New York Assembly. In that body he learned the first lesson of political life: to be effective, a man had to work within the existing system. For the rest of his career he tried to balance the desire for reform and the demand for party regularity, and he succeeded to a remarkable extent.

After a few years in the Assembly, Roosevelt ran for mayor of New York—and finished

"Rough Riders" gather with Theodore Roosevelt in 1898. Roosevelt, as Assistant Secretary of the Navy, had ordered Commodore Dewey to keep his fleet battle-ready for an attack on the Spanish-held Philippines if war broke out. When it did, Roosevelt resigned from his government post and organized the First U.S. Volunteer Cavalry, popularly called the "Rough Riders." Lieutenant Colonel Roosevelt led his troops up the heavily fortified San Juan Hill in Cuba. They took the high ground and brought American artillery to bear on the vulnerable Cuban port of Santiago, where the bottled-up Spanish fleet lay. Proclaimed a hero for his famous charge up San Juan Hill, Roosevelt attracted notice from Republican leaders who needed a popular national figure to share the ticket in 1900 with William McKinley in his bid for another term as President.

third in a three way race! That was to be his last setback for many years. In the meantime, he served as a civil service commissioner, police commissioner of New York, assistant secretary of the Navy, and leader of the Rough Riders. His popularity after the Spanish-American War was so great that he was elected governor of New York in 1899, and then was chosen Vice President.

Theodore Roosevelt was the leader of the liberal "progressive" wing of the Republican Party. At the start of the 20th century, the progressives were just becoming prominent, but they would be in the forefront of American reform movements for many years. To a large extent, they would be responsible for reforming city and state governments, for ending child labor, for pure food and drug legislation, and for the constitutional amendments providing for direct election of senators and suffrage for women.

Among the most important progressives were Robert LaFollette, Hiram Johnson, William Borah, and Albert Cummins. There was also George Norris, who, during his long career in the House and Senate, was responsible for democratizing the rules of the House and for gaining acceptance of public ownership and operation of hydroelectric plants. Today Norris is remembered mostly for the latter success and is known as the father of the Tennessee Valley Authority.

Progressive Republicans did not agree on all issues, but they shared a belief in the propriety of a government active in ensuring the rights of all Americans. Roosevelt held this belief, but he interpreted it in light of his own commitment to leadership. Unlike his predecessors in the White House, Roosevelt felt that the President should lead and Congress follow. And Roosevelt was determined to lead. But he moved slowly at first, in order to get the full support of hesitant party leaders. When he took office, he promised to follow McKinley's policies and carefully avoided antagonizing the old guard.

However, Roosevelt's activist approach was clear almost immediately. His first annual

Energetic campaigner and crusader and a lifelong outdoorsman, Theodore Roosevelt excites a street audience with his characteristic style: high-pitched voice, jutting jaw, and animated gestures. He believed the President should be the "steward of the people," and he boldly led Americans toward progressive reforms and a strong foreign policy. One of his greatest domestic achievements was in the area of conservation. He enhanced Americans' views of their natural heritage by enormously expanding national parks in the West, setting aside other lands for public use, and inaugurating vital irrigation projects.

*"Speak softly and carry a big stick. . . ."
Roosevelt's favorite proverb comes to life in this
cartoon, which shows the President in one of his
favorite roles—"trustbuster." He made it clear
that he would not tolerate illegal monopolies or
any coalition of power that restrained interstate
trade. One of the greatest achievements of his
administration came when a Supreme Court
decision backed his efforts and forced the
dissolution of a great railroad combination in the
Northwest. Under the Sherman Antitrust Act,
other suits followed against monopolies in coal,
oil, tobacco, and other commodities.*

message to Congress provided a catalog of
programs that previewed his activity in the
years to follow. Roosevelt proposed increasing the power of the Interstate Commerce
Commission, changing immigration policy,
increasing trade through reciprocity treaties,
improving working conditions for government employees, building a canal across Central America, enlarging the Navy and Mer-
chant Marine, and creating extensive
conservation programs. The most controversial proposal, one that Roosevelt never was
able to get through Congress, concerned the
regulation of business. His goal was to prevent large business organizations—trusts—
from gaining monopolies and thereby preventing the proper functioning of the free
enterprise system. The new century had
brought not only a new President but also a
new concept of the President's role.

During his first three years in office Roosevelt avoided conflict with the "standpat" conservatives in his party. Yet he still provided
the American people with a vigorous and successful Chief Executive. He gave warning to
businesses to avoid monopolistic practices
through the successful prosecution of the
Northern Securities Company under the Sherman Antitrust Act, winning the title of
"trustbuster." America's working men were
gratified by the President's intervention on
behalf of striking coal miners. Roosevelt recognized the strength of their cause, and aided
them in reaching a settlement resulting in
higher wages and shorter hours.

In 1903 Roosevelt backed revolutionaries
who established the Republic of Panama. Following the revolution, the new Panamanian
government signed a treaty allowing the
United States to build a canal across its territory. The Panama Canal opened in 1914, providing an enormous economic benefit not only
to the United States but also to world trade in
general. Strenuous efforts by Roosevelt succeeded in pushing the Newlands Act through
Congress. The President's love of nature had
given him a strong belief in the importance of
conservation, and the Newlands Act was

First President to leave the soil of the United States during his term of office, Roosevelt visits workmen at Culebra Cut during construction of the Panama Canal. Realizing the growing commercial and political value of the Pacific in world affairs, Roosevelt signed a bill on June 29, 1906, authorizing work to begin on an unparalleled engineering feat—a 40.3-mile-long sea link. The canal—which joins Cristobal on the Caribbean with Balboa, the Bay of Panama terminus—cut passage between the Pacific and Atlantic by 8,000 miles. Voyages that formerly took weeks took only a matter of hours via the strategic waterway.

"Uncle Joe," Joseph G. Cannon of Illinois, wielded his power as Speaker of the House from 1903 to 1911 to make Congress a conservative bastion. Accused of autocratic methods, he ruled by a combination of controlling committee appointments, granting privileges, and presenting a facade of small-town pleasantries. His strong influence over reactionary Republicans forged a formidable wing of opposition to Roosevelt's agenda of progressive reforms. Cannon's conservative ideals aligned him closer to Roosevelt's successor, William Howard Taft.

the first step in the long battle to prevent conscienceless exploitation of America's natural resources.

By the time of the 1904 presidential campaign, Roosevelt was so popular that he won the Republican nomination unanimously. Although accolades in the party's platform must be taken with a grain of salt, the praise given Theodore Roosevelt was a reflection of the image he had achieved in the eyes of the American people: "He had held firmly to the fundamental American doctrine that all men must obey the law; that there must be no distinction between rich and poor, between strong and weak, but that justice and equal protection under the law must be secured to every citizen without regard to race, creed, or condition."

The last phrase was more than just political rhetoric. Roosevelt had earned the hatred of the South by inviting black leader Booker T. Washington to dine at the White House. A few years later he antagonized anti-Semites when he appointed Oscar Straus Secretary of Commerce and Labor. Straus was the first Jew to hold a Cabinet position.

At the time of the election the country was becoming increasingly progressive. The Democrats, however, chose as their nominee an extremely conservative New York judge, Alton B. Parker. Parker could not woo traditionally Republican businessmen from their party, and his conservatism could not compare with Roosevelt's charismatic appeal to the middle classes. The election wasn't even close. Roosevelt won better than 58 percent of the vote and had a margin of 336 to 140 in the electoral college. Parker carried only a dozen southern states, while Roosevelt swept the rest of the country and helped the Republicans to large majorities in both House and Senate.

In his second term as President, Roosevelt emerged as the leader of progressivism and as a major figure on the international scene. With Roosevelt as their patron saint, progressives at all levels won victory after victory. Dozens of states passed laws designed to "give the government back to the people." Direct primaries replaced party conventions, the initiative and referendum forced state legislators to follow the popular will, and the threat of recall hung over the heads of those that refused. Cities replaced mayors with managers or commissions to provide better government. The secret ballot spread like wildfire. These reforms and others owed much to Roosevelt's commitment to greater popular democracy, the "square deal" for all.

At the national level, the President faced strong opposition to many reforms from such conservative congressional leaders as Speaker of the House Joe Cannon and Senators Aldrich and Allison. Through negotiation and compromise, however, Roosevelt was able to push through many of his programs. Conservation laws prevented exploitation of forests, mineral reserves, and water power sites. Antitrust suits kept businesses from creating unfair competitive situations. Business influence over government was limited by a law prohibiting political contributions by corporations. A pure food law and a meat inspection act helped protect public health, and the Hepburn Act allowed the Interstate Commerce Commission to regulate railroad rates.

Roosevelt's impact on foreign policy was as great as it was on domestic affairs. The President recognized that improvements in shipping, the invention of the radio, and the perfection of the telegraph meant a shrinking world. He also knew that a nation as large and powerful as the United States could not remain completely isolated.

The President's success in obtaining the right to build a canal across Panama was only his first step in an extremely activist policy. The countries of Central and South America were plagued by economic and political instability. Some were in danger of defaulting on debts owed to European powers. Americans were worried those powers might invade one or more of the Latin American nations to ensure the debt payments. This would have violated the long-standing American policy of the Monroe Doctrine.

Roosevelt knew something had to be done. He therefore devised his "corollary," or addition, to the Monroe Doctrine: The United States would ensure the debt payments of the Latin American nations. To do this, Roosevelt and his successors sent troops into a number of Caribbean countries. The United States took over and administered the troubled finances of these countries. When the nations' debts were repaid, American forces were withdrawn. Sometimes this policy was abused. The nations to the south disliked America's meddling in their affairs, but at least their independence was preserved.

Roosevelt's vision was not limited to the Western Hemisphere. When Russia and Japan went to war in 1904, Roosevelt sponsored the subsequent peace negotiations that culminated in the Treaty of Portsmouth. For his role as peacemaker, Roosevelt became the first American to win the Nobel Peace Prize. Roosevelt also was responsible for two agreements between the United States and Japan that lessened rivalry between the two nations in the Pacific. Perhaps not accidentally, the second of these agreements followed the arrival in Japan of the Great White Fleet, America's modernized Navy. And the President helped defuse mounting tensions among Europe's imperialist powers in the first Moroccan crisis, which may have delayed the outbreak of World War I.

Roosevelt's accomplishments in domestic and foreign affairs were impressive and substantial. But in the words of historian Elting Morison: "The greater importance of Theodore Roosevelt lies in his efforts to increase his own and his countrymen's understanding of the kind of world they lived in. He was the first President to recognize clearly the meaning of industry. He was the first man in his office to describe clearly not only the problems but the possibilities presented by industrial energy."

In 1908 Roosevelt could have easily won renomination and reelection. But he had promised not to break precedent and seek a third term. Instead, he chose his successor,

LET US HAVE PEACE

W.A.Rogers

Nobel prize winner: Roosevelt prevails on Russia and Japan to end the Russo-Japanese War. He convened a peace conference at Portsmouth, New Hampshire, on August 5, 1905, and, after difficult negotiations, the warring nations signed a treaty on September 5. Roosevelt's mediation efforts won him the world's respect, gratitude, and highest peace award, the Nobel prize.

William Howard Taft. Taft had had a successful career as governor of the Philippines, negotiator with the Japanese, and Secretary of War. With Roosevelt's support, he won the nomination at the Republican convention on the first ballot. The Democrats returned to their old hero, William Jennings Bryan. Benefiting from widespread prosperity and the magic of the Roosevelt connection, Taft won the election handily. Both Houses of Congress were controlled by the Republicans, but the congressional delegation was increasingly split between progressives and conservatives.

From Roosevelt to Warren Harding

Following Theodore Roosevelt, with his colorful and rather spectacular style of leadership, William Howard Taft appeared a somewhat complacent President. This image was unfair, however, since Taft was not unfriendly to moderate reform. In fact, while Roosevelt retained the title of trustbuster, Taft was far more successful than Roosevelt in the enforcement of the antitrust laws. Yet, in politics, the *way* something is done can be almost as important as *what* is done. And Taft's style, in contrast to Roosevelt's, struck many reformers as lackluster.

During Roosevelt's years in the White House, reform had become a respectable goal across the political spectrum. This was the "progressive era," for the Democrats, for the Republicans, and for third parties. It was even possible to claim, as Roosevelt often did, that reform could be viewed as a conservative undertaking, an attempt to preserve social values by adapting them to changing times.

It was perhaps inevitable that a man of Roosevelt's drive would succumb to boredom out of office. In 1910, he returned to the United States from a big-game hunt in Africa to behold the spectacle of Taft's low-key, easy-going manner in the White House. He also beheld the continuing upsurge within the Republican Party of progressive reform sentiment. Especially in Congress, where progressives were challenging the rule of Speaker Joseph Cannon, the impulse for change was evident.

"Vigorous" and "manly" were terms that constantly sprang from the lips of Theodore Roosevelt. It was not long before Roosevelt began to see Taft as a bumbling successor—a leader who could not lead decisively, who was squandering chance after chance to direct the flow of reform. Vigorous reform was imperative in Roosevelt's view. To shirk the call for reform was to risk industrial chaos, the strikes and labor violence that typified the recent past. Preventing a recurrence of this was the duty of all enlightened conservatives, Roosevelt believed. What would happen to the country, he wondered, if Taft should prove to be weak in this regard?

By 1910, Roosevelt began, in the opinion of most of his biographers, to regret his withdrawal from politics. That same year, he issued an important declaration of principles for industrial reform. Moving beyond the terms of his Square Deal policies of past years, Roosevelt issued a call for a "new nationalism." In a shift from his early stance as a trustbuster, Roosevelt had come to believe that combination in industry was both inevitable and desirable. Consolidation bred efficiency and vitality. Antitrust prosecutions could still be used as a last resort to correct industrial abuses, but the essence of Roosevelt's New Nationalism policy was the belief that "bigness" had come to stay in the 20th century.

For this reason, Roosevelt actually took issue with some antitrust prosecutions Taft initiated, such as his prosecution of U.S. Steel. On a host of issues, the former President began to challenge his successor, issues such as Taft's alleged "softness" in the areas of conservation and foreign policy.

Roosevelt was not alone in his criticisms. The election of 1910 had resulted in resounding progressive victories. And yet, the progressives claimed, Taft was all too willing to defer to congressional champions of the old guard, men like Nelson Aldrich, with whom, on the issue of railroad regulation, Roosevelt had sparred in the not too distant past. (A cartoon of the period showed, beneath a glowering portrait of Roosevelt—whose "big stick" was gathering cobwebs—a pathetic Taft, begging and pleading with Aldrich on the issue of tariff reform.)

By 1911, a deep feud had begun to poison

Inspired as a jurist but reserved as a President, William Howard Taft saw his accomplishments in office overshadowed by a raging quarrel between conservative and progressive members of his party. Taft's cautious approach to politics contrasted sharply with Roosevelt's swaggering style of leadership, and he earned scant credit for a number of accomplishments during his administration (1909-13). These included the initiation of 90 antitrust suits, and the submission of amendments to the states for a federal income tax and the direct election of senators. Also during his term, legislation established a postal savings system and directed the Interstate Commerce Commission to set railroad rates.

the once cordial relationship between Taft and Roosevelt. From across the country, progressive Republican leaders began to descend on the Roosevelt home in Oyster Bay. Their message was clear: Theodore Roosevelt was needed as his party's standard-bearer in 1912. At first Roosevelt's reaction seemed to be cool, for there were other contenders who wished to challenge the President. Foremost among them was Robert "Fighting Bob" LaFollette, of Wisconsin. Roosevelt bided his time and followed the currents of public opinion.

All the while, Taft did little to endear himself to Republican progressives. This was a serious blunder. Taft's failure to court the progressives blinded them to his solid accomplishments in office. These achievements included the creation of a postal savings bank and a parcel post, an expansion of the merit system in the post office, the creation of a federal children's bureau, and a special commission of economy and efficiency. Also in the Taft years, the Mann-Elkins Act, which strengthened the Interstate Commerce Commission, was enacted, as were the 16th and 17th Amendments to the Constitution (respectively providing for the federal income tax and the direct election of senators).

Taft was certainly not opposed to reform, but unlike Roosevelt, he was instinctively cautious. He lacked the flair for the dramatic, and he failed to understand the power of symbolism in public life. This often led to misunderstandings. In a famous dispute about conservation policy, Taft felt bound to dismiss the Roosevelt protege Gifford Pinchot as Chief Forester. This was often interpreted among progressives as a sign of retreat from Roosevelt's activism. In fact, though, Pinchot's successor was the head of the Yale School of Forestry, and the Roosevelt conservation policies were actually expanded. But Taft failed to make this point very strenuously, and his image as a traitor to progressive reform was stronger than ever by 1912.

In January of 1912, Roosevelt could wait no longer. Against the advice of intimates like Elihu Root, who feared a battle between

Roosevelt's last major campaign for President, depicted in this 1914 cartoon, split the Republican Party into two camps. At the 1912 Republican presidential nominating convention, when it became apparent that Taft would receive the winning votes, Roosevelt urged his progressive supporters to bolt rather than swing to Taft. After telling a reporter that he felt as "strong as a bull moose," Roosevelt called on his followers to form a third party, the Progressives, popularly known as the Bull Moose Party. With their voting power weakened by the chasm between Taft and Roosevelt, the Republicans lost the 1912 election to the Democratic presidential nominee, Woodrow Wilson. The reform policies of Wilson preempted the need for a Progressive Party. It collapsed in 1916 when Roosevelt declined the Bull Moose nomination for President. His refusal mended the rift that he had caused some four years earlier, and Republicans were able to begin reunifying the party.

Roosevelt and Taft might split the party, Roosevelt declared his intention to seek the Republican nomination. The ensuing battle proved to be all Root had feared. While Roosevelt was vastly popular, Taft was in firm control of the party apparatus. Roosevelt swept to victory in early state primaries, but Taft was able to control the selection of delegates in the many states without primaries. This proved to be decisive.

Roosevelt's supporters made the issue of Taft's alleged ruthlessness a rallying cry. Taft they said, was thwarting the will of the party rank and file, and indeed was virtually stealing the nomination. Roosevelt himself believed this. And when at last the nomination was clearly within Taft's reach, an angry Roosevelt ordered his bloc of delegates to bolt the Republican convention. True to the prophecy of Root, Roosevelt had split the party.

The Republicans nominated Taft to do battle with the Democratic nominee, Woodrow Wilson, but Roosevelt, feeling "strong as a bull moose," was not to be kept from the fray. Along with a number of his ardent followers, Roosevelt founded a third party—the Progressive Party—and championed a platform devoted to the full spectrum of political and social reform: federal regulation of interstate corporate activity, industrial justice, nationwide presidential primaries, electoral review of state judicial decisions, the recall, the initiative, and the referendum. The party itself was a loose coalition of disgruntled followers of Roosevelt, reform idealists, and a few political professionals. In the long run, the breach with the Republican Party was reparable. But as far as the election of 1912 was concerned, the candidacy of Taft was doomed.

The real contest was between Roosevelt and Woodrow Wilson—and their two diverging philosophies. Roosevelt, with his New Nationalism, stood for industrial regulation in an era of big government and big business. A number of important intellectuals, men such as Walter Lippmann and Herbert Croly, supported Roosevelt's point of view. Wilson, under the influence of Louis Brandeis, sought to restore competition through vigorous antitrust policies. Wilson's program was called the New Freedom. In all, the campaign of 1912 was waged upon a very high intellectual plane. The results were unhappy for Taft, who ran third and carried only two states, Utah and Vermont. Wilson, of course, was elected.

During the Wilson years, the first order of Republican business was reunification. Roosevelt kept the Progressive Party alive for a season, but its money and its political strength were running out. Its showing in the 1914 election was poor, and while pressure from the Progressive Party was important in goading Wilson toward an activist program beyond his New Freedom, once goaded, Wilson virtually preempted the field of reform. He, along with the Democratic Congress, lowered the tariff, established the Federal Reserve System and the Federal Trade Commission, and passed more extensive antitrust legislation.

By the 1916 presidential election, however, progressive reform was being eclipsed by developments in foreign policy. This was an area in which, once again, Theodore Roosevelt found himself at odds with a presidential successor. World War I had been raging in Europe since 1914. The manner of America's entry into the war would shatter the progressive movement and profoundly alter the future of the Republican Party.

From the outbreak of the war, Wilson had urged neutrality in thought as well as in action. This was impossible for Theodore Roosevelt, who firmly believed in the Allied cause, who felt a German victory would do incalculable damage to America's national interests, and who viewed war—as he had since his days in the Rough Riders—as a test of manly virtue and courage.

During Wilson's first administration, neutrality proved elusive in any case. Wilson found himself presiding over a vast trade in munitions and armaments, a trade that only the British, with their command of the seas, could use to advantage. The Germans, of course, struck back with the infamous U-boat warfare. Roosevelt urged a severing of U.S.-

German relations because of the U-boats, and he preached preparedness. Wilson also approved a preparedness program by 1916, but he looked upon the war with horror. He sought, through the House-Grey mediation agreement with Great Britain, to forge a negotiated settlement. The Democratic slogan of 1916 was the famous boast: "He kept us out of war." To Theodore Roosevelt, this was nothing to be boasted of at all. He complained (though usually in private) about the "yellowness"—the cowardice—that he felt was undermining America's national strength.

Rhetoric such as that was frightening to Republican leaders in 1916. The country seemed to be overwhelmingly committed to peace. Particularly from midwestern Republicans, warnings were sent to the national leadership that a Roosevelt war-candidacy would trigger yet another party breach, and this the Republican party leaders refused to countenance. The Progressive and Republican conventions met simultaneously in 1916. The Progressives, on the verge of nominating Roosevelt, opened talks with the Republican leaders and learned to their dismay that a Roosevelt candidacy was unacceptable.

At this point, Roosevelt, placing foreign policy above the goals of domestic reform, urged both parties to unite around the nomination of Henry Cabot Lodge, whose conservatism on the issues of domestic reform was equalled by his nationalism on issues of foreign policy. The more idealistic wing of the Progressive Party considered this suggestion insulting. They nominated Roosevelt, who promptly declined the nomination, and with this the Progressive Party effectively collapsed.

The Republicans proceeded to nominate Charles Evans Hughes, a moderate reformer who had served as governor of New York and, since 1910, as an associate justice of the U.S. Supreme Court. (Immediately upon his nomination, Hughes resigned from the Court.) Hughes, like Wilson, was a man of intellectual depth and liberal conviction. His investigations of New York utilities and insurance

First Supreme Court justice chosen as a presidential contender by a major party, Charles Evans Hughes answered his party's call and resigned from the Court to oppose Wilson in 1916. Though a brilliant public servant, Hughes failed to counter the Democrat's platform of progressive reform and peace. Wilson had issued a proclamation of U.S. neutrality at the outbreak of World War I. The appealing slogan, "He kept us out of war," helped keep Wilson in the White House for a second term, although unrelenting submarine warfare against U.S. and Allied ships later convinced Wilson to sign a joint congressional resolution, on April 6, 1917, declaring war against Germany.

companies had made him a hero to progressives. Once pitted against Woodrow Wilson, however, Hughes's ardor for reform appeared to cool significantly. His campaign on the Republican platform of peace, business regulation, conservation, and labor protection was largely negative. When railroad workers threatened to strike on behalf of the eight-hour day—and when the Democrats responded with the Adamson Act, a clear victory for labor—the campaign turned bitter. Hughes attacked the legislation as a surrender to union blackmail. Wilson stoutly defended it. The result was the wholesale defection of many Republican and third-party progressives to the Wilson camp. The Democrats, moreover, used the peace issue to the hilt—and Theodore Roosevelt obliged them, to their delight, by issuing more of his martial declarations.

Finally, like Taft, Hughes did not go out of his way to court individual progressives. For example, Hiram Johnson, the famous progressive Republican governor of California, was waging a difficult fight for a Senate seat amid strong opposition from the California Republican old guard. Once when Hughes and Johnson were staying at the same California hotel, Hughes neglected to call upon the governor, and Republican progressives in California were offended.

The presidential election was close. For a while it appeared Wilson was approaching defeat, but the late returns from the West brought Wilson victory, along with clear indications that progressive reform and peace were indeed the issues that had turned the tide. But in a very few months, on April 6, 1917, peace was irrevocably gone, as America entered the war. American energies were now to be channeled into wartime idealism, wartime mobilization, and wartime intolerance.

The bitterness began quickly. Republican progressives such as Robert LaFollette, who opposed America's entry into the war, were branded traitors. Theodore Roosevelt, in full cry, argued that no respectable position was left for dissenters, that patriotism and stark

sedition were the only real alternatives. War and loyalty—this was now to be the only test of political righteousness.

Rhetoric in both parties became apocalyptic. Everyone, it seemed, considered himself the guardian of national unity, and opponents were simply divisive scoundrels. Wilson declared, for example, in the congressional elections of 1918, that a vote for a Democratic Congress was imperative both to the war effort and to the postwar settlement of Europe. Republicans, of course, considered this to be a low blow. When the electorate returned Republican majorities in both houses of Congress that year, Wilson's tactics returned to haunt him. Republican victories, he had asserted, would amount to a signal to "the other side" that his leadership had been repudiated—and indeed, said Theodore Roosevelt, that was now precisely the case.

This extreme partisanship continued to affect American politics during the peace negotiations at Versailles and during Wilson's struggle to secure ratification of the League of Nations Covenant. Wilson had not invited a single Republican leader of national stature to participate in the treaty negotiations. Moreover, he would brook no compromise at all on the issue of the League, refusing to accept the reservations of Republican leaders such as Henry Cabot Lodge. Consequently, Lodge and Roosevelt became all the more defiantly nationalistic.

Amid the anger and divisions of 1919, the progressive movement was quickly dissolving. Hope had given way to fear, and ideals were lost amid vengeful recriminations. Wilson had suffered a stroke, Roosevelt died of an embolism, and Wilson's Attorney General, A. Mitchell Palmer, unleashed an unprecedented wave of arrests and deportations of radicals and dissenters. A strike by Boston police raised fears of new labor turbulence, and the Republican governor of Massachusetts, Calvin Coolidge, became a hero to many for his firmness in dealing with the strike.

A new era was beginning, an era when Republicans would tacitly disavow the pro-

gressive movement, turning instead to a search for calmness and order in "normalcy." Roosevelt's New Nationalism, a vision of order based upon the power of the state, would give way to Harding, Coolidge, and a return to laissez-faire.

From Harding to Herbert Hoover

The death of Theodore Roosevelt in 1919 robbed the Republican Party of its foremost intellect and leader. Other progressives of comparable intellectual endowment—Robert LaFollette and Hiram Johnson, especially—remained, but without the Roosevelt charisma progressive Republicanism was badly weakened. In 1920, two strong potential presidential candidates, Gen. Leonard Wood and

An embodiment of small-town virtues, Warren G. Harding (seated at right with Henry Ford and Thomas Alva Edison at left) appealed to people weary of war and political turmoil. "America's present need is not heroics, but healing . . . ," he proclaimed. Harding left policy-making mostly to his political machine bosses. His administration eliminated wartime controls, slashed taxes, established a federal budget system, restored the high protective tariff, and imposed strict limitations upon immigration. A booming industry blessed the nation with prosperity during the Harding years. Unfortunately, graft by some of his trusted friends blighted his administration. The biggest scandal since the days of Ulysses S. Grant involved Harding's Secretary of the Interior—Albert B. Fall. In return for bribes, Fall leased drilling rights to a government oil reserve. The scheme became notorious as the Teapot Dome affair.

Governor Frank O. Lowden of Illinois—both moderate-to-liberal—failed to muster enough support to win the Republican nomination. The previous presidential candidate, Charles Evans Hughes, made it clear he was not available. The "available man," to borrow from the title of his best biography, turned out to be a senator and former newspaper editor from Marion, Ohio, Warren Gamaliel Harding. He won the Republican nomination on the tenth ballot. The delegates then selected Calvin Coolidge, the governor of Massachusetts, as their vice presidential nominee.

The Democrats, who nominated James M. Cox and Franklin Delano Roosevelt, sought to make the 1920 election a referendum on the League of Nations. But the actual issues that determined the election were not clear. The Republican platform did not wholeheartedly repudiate the League; the party supported the principle of "an international association," while balking at any "compromise of national independence." More likely, the election turned upon the broader issue of reform, for Harding symbolized retrenchment, and the voters overwhelmingly elected him. The inauguration of 1921—the ailing Wilson giving way to the dapper Harding—seemed to symbolize the end of the progressive movement.

Warren Harding was a vastly popular President. He reminded people of his fellow Ohioan, William McKinley. He was also a contrast—and to many, a pleasant contrast—to Woodrow Wilson and his aloofness. Harding made no pretensions at all toward intellectuality. He sought to inaugurate an era of good feelings. While a man of conservative principles, Harding was usually the first to admit that he was not an original thinker. He intended, simply, to rely upon the men he had appointed to high offices—several of whom were distinguished statesmen, especially Herbert Hoover, who served as his Secretary of Commerce, and Charles Evans Hughes, who accepted the position of Secretary of State.

Had the rest of Harding's appointments been equally distinguished, all might have been well. Under Hughes' guidance, for example, the Harding Administration would sponsor an important naval disarmament conference, the Washington Conference of 1921. But all too often, Harding's appointments were drawn from a circle that (even in Republican quarters) was known as the "Ohio gang." This circle included a number of friends who expected a virtually endless series of favors and special deals. At the dedication of a Harding memorial in 1931, Herbert Hoover would declare: "Warren Harding had a dim realization that he had been betrayed by a few men whom he trusted, by men whom he had believed were his devoted friends. It was later proved in the courts of the land that these men had betrayed not alone the friendship and trust of their staunch and loyal friend, but they had betrayed their country. That was the tragedy of the life of Warren Harding."

The chief offenders were Albert B. Fall, the Secretary of the Interior, Harry Daugherty, the Attorney General, and Charles R. Forbes, the director of the Veterans Bureau. Forbes was convicted of the illegal sale of federal property and went to prison. Daugherty escaped conviction, but was charged by a Senate committee with selling pardons. Fall was convicted in the biggest scandal since the time of Ulysses Grant—the Teapot Dome affair—and was sent to jail. Teapot Dome was the name of a government oil reserve in Wyoming. Fall, in return for bribes, had leased the reserve to the oil company of Harry F. Sinclair. He had also leased the Elk Hill reserve in California to the interest of Edward F. Doheny.

News of the misdeeds had already begun to emerge in 1923 when President Harding died. No one has proven that Warren Harding was himself corrupt. Instead, he appears to have been an instinctively good-hearted person who lacked the resolve to say no to his closest friends.

The Teapot Dome affair was investigated by a Senate committee in the autumn of 1923. Early in the next year, it would dominate headlines for several months. Much of the

Gestures of goodwill by Calvin Coolidge, such as taking off his straw hat to wear the Indian headdress of a Sioux chief, revealed the genuine sense of friendliness and humor that hid behind Coolidge's legendary stern expressions and terse speech. A popular President, Coolidge pursued policies that reflected his New England frugality. He worked to preserve traditional moral and economic precepts amid the material prosperity of the Roaring Twenties. The beneficiary of a soaring economy—"Coolidge Prosperity" some people called it—he favored a marketplace free of government interference. In 1927, during the same vacation trip in which he visited the Sioux Indians in the Black Hills of South Dakota, Coolidge issued the laconic statement: "I do not choose to run for President in 1928."

Engineer, administrator, and humanitarian, Herbert Hoover draws a campaign audience of 22,000 in 1928, the largest political crowd ever gathered in New York to that time. As President, Hoover hoped to usher in a New Era, a period without poverty. But in 1929, the first year of his term, the crash of Wall Street crushed his dreams. He took decisive steps to brace the tottering American financial structure. He fought for a system of home-loan banks, and he created the Reconstruction Finance Corporation. On the other hand, he opposed federal aid to help the thousands of destitute people struck down by the Great Crash. Though people must not suffer from hunger and cold, he said, caring for them must be primarily a matter for private and volunteer charities. Such help was not forthcoming fast enough, and critics made Hoover the scapegoat for the hard times.

important reasons was the character of Harding's presidential successor, Calvin Coolidge. The new President cooperated in the Teapot Dome investigation, which further defused the issue. Here was a man who, in the midst of the Roaring Twenties, symbolized the tradition of New England frugality and thrift. He was a figure of honesty beyond question. Coolidge was not necessarily as humorless a person, however, as he frequently appeared to be. He permitted himself to be crowned with an Indian headdress. He would pose in chaps at a western ranch, with his starched collar and his withering glare in a comic juxtaposition.

Coolidge's politics matched his image: Thrift in government appeared to be the highest attainable good. Republican reformers, however, were left dissatisfied. Though Roosevelt was dead, LaFollete lived. In an effort to rejuvenate the progressive movement, LaFollette broke with the Coolidge Republicans in 1924 in favor of a third-party race. The Democrats, clearly attempting to out-Coolidge Coolidge, nominated John W. Davis, a colorless leader. (The main contenders at the Democratic convention, Alfred E. Smith and William G. McAdoo, arrived at a deadlock because of the intense dispute over Prohibition. Coolidge dodged the Prohibition controversy by limiting himself to the terse observation that existing laws should be enforced.) The election was a landslide victory for Coolidge.

In perilous times, it takes a wise leader to decide whether caution or boldness should carry the day in determining national policy. By the mid-1920s, business was approaching a period of frenzied speculation. But President Coolidge perceived not the slightest danger as the economy became tied to a giddy stock market boom in which American companies were heavily involved in a huge speculative bubble. Cautious Yankee though he was, Coolidge apparently approved of the speculation as a healthy sign of prosperity.

In 1927, in a splendidly typical moment, Coolidge announced with no further comment: "I do not choose to run for President in

resulting uproar was directed at the people who exposed the scandal, Senators Walsh and Wheeler of Montana. The public was unwilling to face any further disillusionment, it seemed, and so the Democratic efforts to turn the scandal to advantage in the 1924 elections proved futile.

Teapot Dome did minimal damage to Republican political fortunes. One of the most

1928." Thus ended a period of Republican history starkly different from the age of Theodore Roosevelt. Coolidge and Roosevelt epitomized the long-standing division over the Republican definition of conservative political philosophy. The creed of Calvin Coolidge was the laissez-faire of the late 19th-century. But an older conception of conservatism, drawn, in part, from the tradition of "noblesse oblige," was the vision of a dynamic government. Thus the New Nationalism announced by Theodore Roosevelt in 1910 was hardly a departure from conservatism. It was only with time that the views Roosevelt bequeathed would be swallowed up by the notion that conservatism and laissez-faire are identical at all times. Even in the 1920s, the change was becoming apparent: What was once called "standpat" conservatism now, for many, symbolized the *only* conservative philosophy.

With Coolidge having removed himself from the field of presidential contenders in 1928, Republicans looked toward Herbert Hoover as his successor. Hoover, who continued to serve as the Secretary of Commerce, was not a career politician at all: He had never before been elected to public office. His fame derived from his various notable achievements. Hoover's extensive travels as an engineer had taken him around the globe, and in the Wilson years he had turned his talents to public service and administration. For example, as chairman of the Commission for Relief in Belgium for four years, he had fed more than ten million people. In 1917, his efficiency was again displayed in his service as wartime Food Administrator. After heading the American Relief Commission in Europe, he stood as a towering humanitarian. Streets were named in his honor throughout Europe.

Hoover is remembered today as a rugged individualist, and so he was. His philosophy was "collective self-help." He opposed any effort to make individuals dependent on government. In other ways, however, he was far more willing than Coolidge to put the energies of government action in those areas where private initiative could not meet the public need:

in flood control, irrigation projects, and basic research. Above all, Herbert Hoover was a manager *par excellence*, and he seemed to be an overwhelmingly capable leader for a technological society.

Hoover won the Republican nomination on the first ballot in 1928. His Democratic opponent was the governor of New York, Alfred E. Smith. The campaign was heated, though Hoover's election was a virtual certainty. A Protestant supporter of Prohibition, Hoover was opposed by a Catholic "wet"—an opponent of Prohibition—heavily involved in the big-city politics of Tammany Hall. Hoover was elected by a wide margin, but Democratic strength was improving among blacks and foreign-born voters, a fact whose significance was yet to be fully understood.

Hoover was a man of ideals, and he hoped to usher in a New Era, a period of abundance in which poverty would be eliminated. But within the first year of his term the most disastrous financial panic in American history burst the stupendous bubble of Wall Street. The effects of the Great Crash would be terrible and far-reaching.

At first, the Depression appeared to be manageable. America had always recovered from hard times before. And with the vast productive potential of modern industry, Hoover believed the economy would quickly recover, if confidence could be restored. But the economy did not recover. In part, as Hoover was quick to point out, an international reaction was taking place, for by the summer of 1931, European banks were calling in their American loans and contracting the chain of credit.

The American economy was settling toward paralysis. Businessmen, in their haste to make good on the borrowed funds lost in the Great Crash, were laying off workers and, in turn, shrinking the mass market. Unemployment spread, consumption dropped, and the wealthy were hardly eager to risk their funds in producing goods that consumers could not buy.

Horrendous communities began to appear

amid city dumps, where people were suddenly reduced to existing in shacks and in cardboard boxes. The communities were all too frequently called by a common name— Hoovervilles. The poignancy of Hoover's position was reflected in former President Harry Truman's remarks at the dedication of the Herbert Hoover Library in West Branch, Iowa, on August 10, 1962: "He did a job . . . that nobody else in the world could have done. He kept millions of people from starving to death after the Second World War just as he did after the First World War. . . . And when I asked him if he would be . . . willing to do the job he

A free soup kitchen in 1930 helps feed jobless victims of the Great Depression. The collapse of European economies in 1931 caused European banks to call in their American loans, forcing U.S. banks in turn to demand payment of domestic loans. This chain of pressure plunged the nation into even deeper depression. Unemployment rose, stock prices and production fell, business failures multiplied, and fear and suffering stalked the country. For the party in office, the Great Depression spelled disaster. Blocs of Republican voters began to turn to the Democrats for a new deal, ushering in 20 years of Democratic domination of national politics.

never hesitated one minute. He said, yes, Mr. President, I'll do it. And he did. . . ."

In truth, Hoover, more than any other President before him, took decisive action to end an economic depression. He fought for a system of home-loan banks, and he created the Reconstruction Finance Corporation to save the tottering American financial structure. But on the question of direct relief, he was adamant: Relief was a matter for private charity in coordination with state and local government. Federal aid to individuals, he said, would establish a bureaucratic tyranny.

The President insisted that if local and private relief should fail, then the federal government would act. But he never saw fit to declare that this moment was at hand. He firmly believed the economy would soon recover, and the bitter jests of an increasingly hostile public stung the man who had only campaigned for office once in his life, and who lacked the ability to sway the crowd or to rise to the public occasion. Though Hoover's opponent in 1932, Franklin Delano Roosevelt, was equally committed to government frugality, Hoover's political fate was all but sealed. The election of 1932 would prove to be a turning point for America. The Republican ascendancy was soon to be shattered for 20 years.

The Loyal Opposition: Hoover to Eisenhower

From the time that Franklin D. Roosevelt entered the White House in 1933 to the onset of World War II, his abiding goal was economic recovery. Heavily defeated in the 1932 elections, the Republican Party could do little but lick its wounds and pledge whatever form of opposition or approval seemed appropriate. FDR was viewed in such a patriotic light that it made little sense for Republicans to openly defy him. Most of his early New Deal program was passed in a congressional whirlwind known as the Hundred Days.

It is difficult today to reconstruct the atmosphere of 1933, when even sober tycoons were so alarmed at the social unrest surrounding them that they openly discussed the possibility of class war. In such an atmosphere, business was eager to lend its support to the President's emergency program. Roosevelt intended to stabilize the economic situation by closing the banks temporarily—to break the cycle of runs on banks—and by encouraging industrywide cooperation of labor and management through the National Recovery Administration codes. This emergency program did not really seem more radical than anything conceived in an earlier age by the President's distant cousin, Theodore Roosevelt.

Controversies began in 1934 and 1935, when FDR began to experiment with curing the Depression through public works programs: the Civil Works Administration, the Works Progress Administration, the Public Works Administration, the Civilian Conservation Corps. In part, this approach was based on the presidential pledge of "bold, persistent experimentation" to promote recovery. The Depression was lingering on, and so the President was changing his tactics. But something else was involved. In 1934 and '35, a host of radical voices could be heard demanding a vigorous "sharing of the wealth," and against this background—created by men like Huey Long, Father Charles Coughlin, and Francis Townsend, all accused of being demagogues— the President swung to the left with a more populistic program. Huey Long was assassinated in 1935, but his successor, the anti-Semitic Gerald L.K. Smith, joined Father Coughlin in supporting Representative William Lemke of North Dakota as the radical Union Party candidate for President in 1936.

Despite the power these radicals seemed to command, conservatives opposed FDR's new programs with increasing vehemence. The Liberty League, composed of implacable business opponents of activist government, condemned the President for carrying the nation toward socialism. By 1936 the climate was so bitter that, in the words of historian Richard Hofstadter, FDR came to feel, "The people who were castigating him were muddle-headed ingrates. During the campaign of 1936 he compared them to the old man saved from drowning who berated his rescuer for not salvaging his hat. . . ." Consequently, in the 1936 campaign the President indulged in his famous rhetorical attacks on "economic royalists" and the "forces of selfishness and lust for power," while his various opponents condemned him in turn for becoming a dictator.

Throughout the first four years of the FDR presidential era, Republicans varied in their responses to "that man in the White House." Some, like the old progressives Hiram Johnson and George W. Norris, openly supported Roosevelt on most issues, as did Robert LaFollette, Jr., the son of "Fighting Bob." Others, defiant to the end, talked of nominating Hoover again, though defeat would have been a certainty. Many supported the Liberty League and longed for a return to the policies of Calvin Coolidge, now in his grave. But the Republican rank and file seemed to lean toward moderate candidates and leaders in a time of bewildering change and diminished power.

Thus Alfred M. Landon, the moderate governor of Kansas, was chosen as the Republican standard-bearer in 1936. A cautious progressive, Landon campaigned on a platform devoted to "the welfare of American men and women" and "their character as free citizens, which today for the first time are threatened by the government itself." The Republican platform assailed the growing centralization of government while nonetheless accepting a number of New Deal objectives in principle— relief, old-age security, and full employment in particular.

The Democrats, however, were in full cry, and the undeniable Roosevelt magnetism was bolstered by a new demographic strategy. Through this strategy, the Democrats dissolved old regional party ties in favor of interest-group appeal, targeted to laborers, farmers, blacks, and urban ethnics. The election, the greatest landslide yet to occur in American politics, amounted to a huge Democratic sweep. Roosevelt carried every state but Vermont and Maine.

Kansas Governor Alfred M. Landon and running mate Frank Knox carried Republican hopes of victory into the 1936 campaign against Democratic incumbent Franklin Delano Roosevelt. Friendly, but lacking dramatic flair, Landon appealed to middle-of-the-road Republicans who wanted a candidate who had not been in the spotlight of national controversy. Landon's call for balanced budgets and moderately progressive governmental action went almost unheard in the whirlwind of FDR's rhetoric to special interest groups, such as laborers, farmers, and blacks. For the first time in U.S. politics, this election saw a clear majority of northern blacks vote for a Democratic candidate for President.

"We want Willkie," chanted Republican delegates at the 1940 presidential nominating convention in Philadelphia. Wendell Willkie embraced a platform that largely agreed with Roosevelt's New Deal theme. Willkie argued, however, that the Republicans could run the recovery program more efficiently. American voters did not agree. FDR remained in the White House in 1941 for an unprecedented third term.

Despite the Democratic landslide, Roosevelt's second term would witness the beginnings of a Republican revival. The President himself was, to a certain extent, responsible for this, for in his mounting frustration with those who opposed his reforms, he proposed what would come to be known as his "court-packing" scheme of 1937. Much New Deal legislation had been thwarted by a group of Supreme Court conservatives. Roosevelt, buoyed by his triumph at the polls, proposed a new plan of "reform." For every justice who had served over ten years and who refused to retire at 70, a new justice—up to a maximum of six—might now be appointed by the President.

Within days of his announcement, it was clear the President had overplayed his hand. Cries of opposition to Roosevelt's "dictatorial" policies arose from almost every quarter. Republicans and southern and western Democrats condemned the plan as a disruption of checks and balances. By summer, the proposal was dead, defeated by a vote of 10-8 in the Senate Judiciary Committee.

Meanwhile, the Depression continued, and New Deal programs, though they did alleviate misery, never succeeded in restoring America to prosperity, full employment, or a healthy level of consumption. Tragically, it took the mobilization during World War II to sufficiently "prime the pump" of the American economy. The issues of war and peace would dominate American politics during Roosevelt's second term. The rise of totalitarian power abroad was a challenge to American democracy. Roosevelt believed that the aggressive fury of the Axis powers should be checked through collective security. Others believed that security must lie in America's isolated strength, and that any foreign intervention amounted to a dance of death.

The isolationists feared that attempts to deter European or Asian aggression would amount to a repetition of the "entangling alliances" that led to World War I. Collective security, they felt, implied a refusal to learn from the past, a refusal to learn that the surest security was in minding one's own business. Roosevelt, however, believed that if appeasement of Hitler and the Axis continued, then democracies would find themselves alone in a tyrannized world, or as Winston Churchill feared, in a new "dark age."

Republicans and Democrats alike were divided between isolationist and internationalist points of view. The President's political position was becoming precarious. Western progressives who supported New Deal reform were rather frequently isolationist, and, conversely, the southern conservatives resistant to domestic reform were often internationalist. To keep the support of internationalists in foreign policy, Roosevelt was increasingly forced to retreat on domestic reform.

Republicans were equally divided into tense and shifting coalitions. Supporters of Hoover had not been sympathetic to Landon's concessions to reform in 1936, and yet Landon's faction retained sufficient power to effectively sidetrack Hoover's suggestion of a midterm policy convention in 1938. The elections of 1938 propelled the fortunes of two rising Republican stars: Thomas E. Dewey, the tough New York DA whose war on crime had achieved national attention and who narrowly lost his bid for the New York governorship, and Robert A. Taft, son of the late President, who was elected to the Senate from Ohio. Both men were mentioned in connection with the 1940 presidential nomination. So were the isolationist Arthur H. Vandenberg, Senator from Michigan, and Wendell Willkie, a political novice whose fame derived from his career as a Wall Street lawyer defending utilities.

Wendell Willkie, however cautiously, aligned himself with the Republican internationalists, while Dewey and Taft were less willing to offend the isolationists. Willkie, the dark horse amateur, exerted a magnetic appeal. At the Republican convention in Philadelphia, Willkie won the presidential nomination on the sixth ballot as his fervent supporters chanted "We want Willkie" from the galleries of the packed convention hall.

Charles L. McNary, the minority leader of the Senate, was chosen as the nominee for Vice President.

In the 1940 campaign, both FDR and Willkie labored under serious handicaps. Roosevelt was seeking to shatter the sanctified two-term tradition in American politics, and once again the cries of "dictator" swelled against him. Willkie, however, was running an essentially "me too" campaign. He sincerely agreed with Roosevelt in foreign policy and accepted in principle much of the New Deal program while arguing that inefficiency had marred its effectiveness. In other words, Republicans could do it better, Willkie was saying.

Willkie's position was a far cry indeed from the philosophy of Calvin Coolidge in the 1920s. Though Willkie succeeded to a greater extent than had any Republican presidential candidate since 1928, the election of 1940 was another Democratic victory. Roosevelt's continuing popularity was strengthened by a number of canny moves, including the appointment of two prominent Republicans—Henry Stimson and Frank Knox—to Cabinet positions, as Secretary of War and Secretary of the Navy respectively. Though Republicans gained a few seats in the Senate, the Democrats controlled Congress. Such was America's political situation a year before Pearl Harbor.

With the coming of war, Americans closed ranks, with the exception of a group of isolationist leaders who disagreed with the strategy of pressing for a victory in Europe before defeating Japan. Otherwise, Republicans and Democrats united around the wartime leadership of FDR, while reserving the right to disagree on domestic issues. These issues were apparently important enough to give Republicans sizable gains in the 1942 midterm elections, including the election of Thomas E. Dewey to the governorship of New York.

Philosophically, Republicans were led by a spirit of moderation in the early 1940s. Increasingly, Republicans began to question isolationist leaders. In 1943, the internationalism

Republican campaign buttons for 1948 touted New York Governor Thomas E. Dewey for President and Earl Warren for Vice President. Four years earlier, as the Republican choice for President, Dewey had boldly pointed Republicans away from isolationism toward active U.S. participation in international affairs. On domestic issues he, like Willkie, agreed with Roosevelt's New Deal while criticizing its specific policies. Roosevelt's leadership, Dewey maintained, ". . . has been consistently hostile to and abusive of American business and American industry. . . ." Nevertheless, Dewey proved no match for FDR, who easily won another term in 1944, his fourth. But on April 12, 1945, Roosevelt suddenly died in office. His Vice President, Harry S. Truman, served out the term and ran against Dewey for a second term in 1948. Opinion polls showed Truman trailing Dewey. Convinced that Dewey had won, newspapers shouted out his victory in large headlines. But the next day, when all electoral votes had been counted, Truman came out on top with a stunning upset.

of Wendell Willkie was popularized through the publication of his book, *One World*. That same year a Republican Postwar Advisory Council approved in principle a postwar league for preventing future aggression, and the party's platform affirmed this principle in 1944.

Willkie, to prove the new acceptance of collective security among Republicans, entered the Wisconsin presidential primary in 1944 espousing the principles of "one world." He hoped, in a historically isolationist state, to achieve a political tour de force. But he attempted too much and was badly defeated. His Wisconsin defeat, however, while fatally crippling his chances for the 1944 presidential nomination, did not seriously damage the cause of Republican internationalism, as the candidacy of Thomas Dewey was to prove. Dewey and his running mate, Senator John W. Bricker of Ohio, achieved the nomination on the first ballot without any major opposition.

Like Willkie, Dewey was, with increasing boldness, ready to accept an internationally active role for the United States. "We are agreed," he said, "all of us, that America will participate with other sovereign nations in a cooperative effort to prevent future wars." On domestic issues, Dewey was in sympathy with Roosevelt's goals, while severely critical of his specific policies. "We Republicans," he said, "are agreed that full employment shall be a first objective of national policy," but Roosevelt's leadership had "lived in chattering fear of abundance. . . . It has been consistently hostile to and abusive of American business and American industry. . . ."

But Dewey was not the campaigner Willkie had been. Despite reports that the President's health was failing, Roosevelt, along with his newest running mate, Harry Truman of Missouri, swept to yet another victory. Democrats also retained majorities in both houses of Congress. Roosevelt, however, died only three months after his fourth inauguration, and Harry Truman, a political unknown, inherited the policies of New Deal reform and international collective security that Roosevelt had pioneered.

Though Truman was to prove a most resourceful politician and leader, Republican fortunes were rising as World War II was brought to a victorious end. For as wartime price controls were lifted, a ruinous inflation, together with commodity shortages and strikes, eroded Democratic strength. At last, it seemed, the political pendulum was swinging to the Republican side, as the 1946 midterm elections gave control of both houses of Congress to the GOP—the first time this had occurred since the election of 1928.

Joseph Martin was the new Republican Speaker of the House, and his second-in-command was Charles W. Halleck, recently converted from isolationism. Immediate tension infused presidential-congressional relations when the new Republican Congress took office. In 1947, Republican leaders and the President feuded over labor policy as Congress passed the controversial Taft-Hartley Act over Truman's veto. The act, intended to curtail what its authors viewed as labor union excesses, prohibited the closed shop and provided for a 60-day cooling off period in major strikes.

The impressive GOP victories of 1946, and the inauspicious wrangling that seemed to have stymied President Truman's domestic program, convinced Republicans that 1948 would be their year of triumph. The Democrats were badly divided by splits into third and fourth parties: Henry A. Wallace, Vice President during Roosevelt's third term, revived the progressive standard and ran for President, demanding civil rights legislation, public ownership of basic industry, and a negotiated peace with the Soviets; Governor Strom Thurmond of South Carolina opposed all centralized government and ran as the States' Rights candidate.

Given the Democrats' contention and division, the Republican nomination of 1948 was an eagerly sought prize. Thomas Dewey, who had been reelected governor of New York in 1946, was convinced his moment was at hand.

Senator Taft sought to campaign on a promise of federal aid in the "necessities of life." Harold Stassen, a former Minnesota governor who had served in the Navy, was another of the major contenders. The field also included such leaders as Senator Arthur Vandenberg, California Governor Earl Warren, Joseph Martin, the genial Speaker of the House, and the war hero, Gen. Douglas MacArthur.

Stassen was the early leader in the state primaries. Dewey decided to challenge Stassen directly in Oregon, a challenge that led to a notable radio debate and a vigorous statewide tour. Dewey's victory in Oregon put him in the lead, and at the national convention he received the nomination on the third ballot, the first time in history Republicans turned to a defeated nominee as their standard-bearer. With Earl Warren as his running mate, Dewey committed the Republican Party once again to a progressive and activist platform. President Truman, far behind in the polls, challenged the Republican Congress to enact its own platform in a summer session, but Republican leaders refused to rise to the bait. And so Truman launched a "whistle-stop" campaign, castigating "do-nothing" Republican leaders and policies.

The election, of course, was one of the greatest political upsets in history, with Truman carrying 28 states to Dewey's 16. Though the Republican electoral vote was the largest since 1928, the party lost control of Congress. What could have accounted for the outcome? No doubt the personal factor was crucial, for Harry Truman ran a feisty campaign that appealed to Americans' love of the underdog. He had, in the parlance of the times, "moxie." Dewey's campaigning, by contrast, proved to be overconfident and dull.

Demographic changes were also important, for the Democratic inroads among urban, ethnic, labor, and farm blocs were of great importance in extending the party's strength. However controversial the tenets of New Deal policies, the Democrats had largely reshaped America's political and social landscape. The welfare state was a creation that few of the

Supreme Commander of the Allied Expeditionary Forces, Gen. Dwight D. Eisenhower demands "Full victory—nothing else" of his troops on the eve of the Normandy invasion, June 6, 1944. A national hero after World War II, Eisenhower was asked by both Republicans and Democrats to bear their standard. He declined, but in 1952 he declared himself a moderate Republican and carried his party to its first national victory in nearly a quarter-century.

major Republican leaders were willing to challenge in the late '40s.

Changes, however, were brewing and would quickly materialize. Tensions between America and Russia had already hardened into cold war confrontations in Greece, in Iran, and in Berlin. The fear of an atomic war was an increasingly pervasive factor in American life after Russia acquired the bomb. A shooting war in Korea added to the tension

calming leader, a military hero who commanded instinctive trust. The extraordinary struggle between these forces would determine the immediate future of Republicanism in the 1950s.

The Age of Eisenhower

In 1948, both major parties approached Gen. Dwight D. Eisenhower as a presidential prospect. "Ike," as the general was known, had been Supreme Allied Commander in Europe during World War II. The tradition of generals becoming involved in politics dated back to the time of Washington and Jackson, and seasoned politicians were convinced that he could easily win. But Eisenhower politely declined in favor of service to education, briefly serving as president of Columbia University. He then returned to active military duty as commander of NATO.

Despite the upset victory of Truman in the 1948 election, the Democrats continued to be vexed by problems, chiefly a flurry of corruption—none of which involved the President—and anxieties related to the cold war with the Soviet Union. The case of Alger Hiss, a high-ranking State Department official accused of espionage, and the outbreak of war in Korea fueled the anxieties. Though Truman's decision in 1950 to send American troops to oppose the invasion of South Korea was hailed by leaders of both parties, the war became something of a stalemate. Moreover, Truman's dismissal for insubordination of Gen. Douglas MacArthur, a flamboyant officer, was a cause of further malaise. All this led to what would soon become known as the "McCarthy era."

and alarm, as did the concern among a number of political leaders over communist subversion in the U.S.

By 1950, Americans were frightened and troubled. Two Republican leaders, Senator Joseph R. McCarthy of Wisconsin and Gen. Dwight D. Eisenhower, would respond to that fear, though in radically different ways. McCarthy, a leader whose very political identity was based on fear, would be opposed by a

On February 9, 1950, in Wheeling, West Virginia, Senator Joseph McCarthy claimed he had proof that the State Department was infiltrated by communists. Thus began a four-year cycle of accusations that would test Republican principles. Not a single one of McCarthy's accusations or implications would be verified, but his power would become immense,

Popular President and First Lady, Ike and Mamie lived happily in the White House for eight years. The Eisenhowers entertained an unprecedented number of heads of states and foreign dignitaries, and Mamie's graciousness endeared her to her guests and to the public. Ike's appeal transcended his image as military hero; to many people he exemplified American decency and simplicity.

largely because of his ability to garner headlines. His mere displeasure would eventually be cause for dismissal of government employees as so-called "security risks." He even smeared loyal officers like Gen. George Marshall, who had served as Truman's Secretary of State. But McCarthy's power in Republican circles would eventually be curtailed.

The fight for the Republican nomination in 1952 was hotly contested. Senator Robert Taft was the first choice of many conservative Republicans who balked at yet another liberal candidacy such as those of Willkie and Dewey. Governor Dewey, however—still a force in the party—warned against neglecting the urban centers of Democratic strength. The Dewey faction united around the candidacy of Eisenhower, who had recently revealed his political affiliation and philosophy: moderate Republican.

Eisenhower won the nomination after bitter credentials fights with Taft delegations from the South. Senator Richard M. Nixon, prominent in anticommunist circles, was first on Eisenhower's list of acceptable running mates, and he was duly selected by acclamation as the vice presidential nominee. The Democrats nominated Adlai Stevenson, the witty and liberal governor of Illinois.

The campaign was marred by controversies over Senator Nixon's finances, but the vice presidential candidate effectively defused the charges in his famous "Checkers" television speech. Television had now come into its own as a factor in national campaigns. The election results were a personal triumph for Eisenhower: He had won 39 states to Stevenson's nine. The long hiatus was over, and Republicans at last could rejoice: They had recaptured the White House. Eisenhower, however, ran far ahead of his party, for Republicans achieved only slight majorities in Congress.

Dwight Eisenhower's appeal transcended his role as a military hero. To many, he was a symbol of American decency and simplicity. Although some of his policies as President appeared to his critics to be inarticulate, recent appraisals have credited Eisenhower with shrewdness. He achieved his goals indirectly and without fanfare—a subtle and effective approach, perhaps, in an age of anxiety. But above all, Eisenhower the soldier and citizen proved to be a man of peace. His moderate policies combined internationalism and humanitarian concern with caution and fiscal restraint.

Eisenhower delicately sought to keep America secure while avoiding conflict or huge military budgets. In "The Chance for Peace," a speech he delivered in 1953 to the American Society of Newspaper Editors, he said: "Every gun that is made, every warship launched, every rocket fired signifies in the final sense a theft from those who hunger and are not fed, those who are cold and are not clothed. This world in arms is not spending money alone. It is spending the sweat of its laborers, the genius of its scientists, the hopes of its children. . . . This is not a way of life

. . . under the cloud of war, it is humanity hanging from a cross of iron."

Upon taking office in 1953, Eisenhower took steps to bring the Korean War to a negotiated end. He avoided direct involvement in the conflicts of French Indo-China (Vietnam) in the years that followed. And in a 1955 summit meeting with the Soviet leaders at Geneva, he advanced his famous "open skies" proposals, calling for reciprocal U.S.-Soviet aerial inspections of military sites as a step towards arms limitation. Unfortunately, the Soviet response was negative.

Eisenhower's immediate concerns, however, were centered on Joseph McCarthy, a man who threatened to destroy any climate of benign moderation in America. As far as historians can tell, Eisenhower's low-key strategy was based upon the confidence that McCarthy's recklessness would lead to his own undoing. This proved to be the case. When McCarthy broadened his accusations to include the Department of the Army, Republicans began to question his goals. The result was the famous series of televised Army-McCarthy hearings of 1954, in which the true back-alley savor of McCarthyism appeared. And as the hearings concluded, Republican Senator Ralph Flanders of Vermont moved that the Senate formally censure McCarthy for his conduct. On December 2, 1954, the Senate "condemned" McCarthy by a vote of 67 to 22, and McCarthy's career as a demagogue was over. He died in comparative obscurity in 1957.

Meanwhile, the moderate brand of Republicanism espoused by Eisenhower continued to develop, along with an easygoing presidential style. Eisenhower's chief Republican rival, Senator Robert Taft, had died in 1953, and the President's own declining health led to cautious leadership. Most of the President's day-to-day decisions were channeled through his special assistant, the former governor of New Hampshire, Sherman Adams. The dominant figure in the Cabinet was John Foster Dulles, the Secretary of State. A militant anticommunist, Dulles had unique access to the President. Historians are still debating who was the stronger figure in formulating foreign policy.

Eisenhower's staff system was designed to shelter him from tedious details and political pressures. His penchant for delegating authority could place extraordinary powers in the hands of subordinates. And yet, historians today are increasingly convinced that in essential matters the President always prevailed and that highly visible figures like Dulles served as "lightning rods" to permit him to formulate his policies quietly, behind the scenes.

The midterm elections of 1954 left Congress with slight Democratic majorities, which further increased the need for political statesmanship. Congress proceeded to raise the minimum wage and voted funds for increasing the availability of the new polio vaccine. While hardly a militant advocate of laissez-faire, Eisenhower sought to keep further extensions of the welfare state to a minimum. Businessmen dominated Cabinet positions and federal regulatory commissions, and a number of presidential decisions reflected a suspicion of activist government: Federal rights to offshore oil were increasingly returned to the states; federal pollution control programs were vetoed; proposed expansions of public power through programs like TVA were decisively blocked. (The President, however, resisted proposals to sell the TVA to private industry.)

Working with the Congress and fellow Republicans, President Eisenhower instituted one of the greatest building projects in any administration: the Interstate Highway System. The outstanding characteristic of the interstate system is its magnitude. Today, all of the planned 43,000 miles have been built and are being used. The system has proven to be the largest public works project in the history of the world, exceeding even the construction of the Panama Canal. Tremendous reductions in fuel consumption, pollution, and automotive maintenance costs have resulted from the highway system's efficiency. There is little doubt that Americans have benefited more from the 100 billion dollar investment in the

interstate system than from any other investment, except that in education. The documented value of the benefits already totals some 500 billion dollars, and benefits are piling up daily.

Another milestone of the Eisenhower Administration occurred on July 10, 1954, when the President signed Public Law 480— the renowned Food for Peace Program,

President Eisenhower addresses the Congress; behind him sits Vice President Richard M. Nixon. In his talks to Congress and the nation, Eisenhower stressed peace, prosperity, and progress. Those ingredients formed the core of Republican arguments for his reelection in 1956. Ike achieved his goals with an easygoing style of leadership that projected a calming influence in an age of anxiety. Among his notable accomplishments in office, Eisenhower signed the strongest civil rights legislation passed since 1875. The Civil Rights Act of 1957 provided for federal prosecution of violators of voting rights and created a commission on civil rights. Ike also instituted one of the greatest achievements in any administration: the Interstate Highway System. The 43,000-mile network exceeds the construction of the Panama Canal as the largest public works project in history.

acclaimed as one of the great humanitarian acts performed by one nation for the needy of the world. By 1984, the 30th anniversary of the Food for Peace Program, the United States had shipped more than 300 million tons of agricultural products, valued at 33 billion dollars, to more than a hundred countries. The shipments of surplus food totaled 3.4 million tons the first year; two years later they reached the level of 14 million tons, and eventually averaged ten million tons a year.

The Eisenhower Food for Peace Program, however, is more than a humanitarian act. It has become the most effective U.S. agricultural program in history, underpinning the success and income of American farmers. It is the most effective economic development program ever offered by one nation to build and rebuild the economies of other nations. It is the most effective long-term program ever devised to stimulate trade between nations. And it is responsible for helping make the United States the number one agricultural exporter in the world by a wide margin.

Though President Eisenhower suffered a heart attack in 1955, he recovered sufficiently to answer his party's call for renomination in 1956. Some Republican leaders such as Harold Stassen believed the combative political tactics of Vice President Nixon were becoming a liability. Stassen tried to organize a movement to replace Nixon on the ticket with moderate Governor Christian A. Herter of Massachusetts. But the movement ended when Herter announced he would place Nixon's name in nomination for the vice presidency. The Eisenhower-Nixon team was renominated on the first ballot, and the Democrats again chose Adlai Stevenson as their candidate.

The Republican platform stressed the Eisenhower record of peace and prosperity, enshrining the Eisenhower creed of humanitarianism and fiscal caution: "In all those things which deal with people, be liberal, be human. In all those things which deal with people's money, or their economy, or their form of government, be conservative."

The major campaign issues revolved

around Stevenson's proposals to abolish the peacetime draft and abandon the testing of large nuclear weapons. Though Eisenhower stressed his record, the biggest Republican advantage in 1956 was the vast popularity of Eisenhower himself. "I Like Ike," the informal Republican rallying cry, said all that was needed about the President's image of benevolence and honesty.

Eisenhower's victory in 1956 was even more decisive than his triumph of 1952: The electoral vote was 457 for Eisenhower to 73 for Stevenson. Yet the Democrats continued to maintain slim majorities in Congress. And changes were developing that soon would mean trouble for the age of equilibrium Eisenhower hoped to establish. The movement for black civil rights, which can be traced to the program of the Radical Republicans during Reconstruction, surged to the fore as a major national issue in the 1950s.

The civil rights issue, essentially, concerned whether the intent of the Reconstruction amendments to the Constitution would be fulfilled. Already, in the famous 1954 Supreme Court decision of *Brown v. Board of Education of Topeka*—a unanimous decision written by the new Republican chief justice and former California governor, Earl Warren—the Court had reversed the doctrine of "separate but equal" and proclaimed that school segregation violated the constitutional guarantee of equal protection under the law.

That decision was put to a test in 1957, when Governor Orval E. Faubus of Arkansas attempted to obstruct desegregation of schools in Little Rock. On September 24, President Eisenhower dispatched federal troops to the city to protect black children from mobs and to enforce federal court desegregation orders. That same year, Congress passed the strongest civil rights legislation since Reconstruction, providing for federal prosecution of those who violated voting rights and creating a federal commission on civil rights to monitor the situation.

Yet another event in 1957 added sudden excitement to the national political scene: the

launching of the satellite *Sputnik I* by the Soviet Union. Soviet premier Nikita Khrushchev made the most of the achievement with broad claims of Soviet technical superiority. Americans, accustomed to technological preeminence, reacted with dismay. The military issue was also a factor, for the Soviet achievement hinted at strategic breakthroughs and missiles capable of delivering a nuclear strike from across the globe.

The "space race" was on, and the initial American efforts were disappointing. The Vanguard satellite program was a failure for months on end, as one rocket after another went up in flames at Cape Canaveral. Eventually the Army succeeded in launching a satellite in 1958, but the public was alarmed. Questions arose as to how far behind the Russians America could be, and demands for more aid to education were heard in Congress.

Space race jitters, combined with an economic recession in 1957, led to significant Democratic victories in the midterm elections

Breaking school segregation in the South, black students arrive for class in Little Rock, Arkansas. In 1957 the state's governor, Orval E. Faubus, ordered National Guard troops to "protect" Little Rock's all-white high school. The action defied a federal court desegregation order by preventing nine black students from attending the first day of classes. The federal court ordered the governor to recall the National Guard. The ruling touched off rioting. To protect the black children from angry mobs and to enforce the court's desegregation order, President Eisenhower dispatched 1,000 paratroopers of the 101st Airborne Division to Little Rock. The President also exercised his constitutional authority by placing the Arkansas National Guard under federal command. On September 25, with their safety secured, the black students entered the high school for its first day of integrated classes.

of 1958. One of the major Republican triumphs was the victory of Nelson Rockefeller in the race for the New York governorship, but Rockefeller's liberal views were yet another indication that the country desired a change.

To a degree the administration and congressional leaders responded to this desire for change. The long-delayed admission of Alaska and Hawaii to statehood, the creation of the National Aeronautics and Space Administration, and the passage of a National Defense Education Act, which provided millions of dollars for student loans in linguistic and scientific studies, stand as bipartisan achievements of Eisenhower's second term. While Eisenhower strove to keep America abreast of technological developments, he nonetheless warned the country against the danger of a "military-industrial complex" arising from the cold war.

The Eisenhower years had been a time of peace and prosperity under tranquil leadership. However, in 1960 Americans could sense that a decade of change was impending. The political disgrace of McCarthy and Stevenson's inability to wrest the presidency from Republican control had left Eisenhower as the dominant political figure throughout the '50s. But Democratic leaders, in their scramble for the 1960 presidential nomination, were already vying with each other's programs. A welter of contenders was waiting in the wings, and the election of 1960 would prove to be a cliff-hanger.

An Age of Confrontations: 1960–1972

Each of the contenders for the Democratic nomination of 1960—Adlai Stevenson, John F. Kennedy, Lyndon Johnson, Stuart Symington, Wayne Morse, Hubert Humphrey—challenged the Eisenhower record. Kennedy, the young Massachusetts senator who triumphed at the Democratic convention, made it clear: His was to be a campaign of youth, and he asserted that more "vigor" was needed both in cold war struggles and in domestic issues such as civil rights.

The Republican front-runner, Vice President Nixon, defended the Eisenhower record and stressed his own experience, contrasted with Kennedy's brief career. Nixon's only serious competition for the nomination was the newly elected Republican governor of New York, Nelson Rockefeller. Though Rockefeller had announced in 1959 that he would not be a presidential candidate, he secretly retained this ambition and quietly sounded out Republican leaders across the country. But the response was disappointing: Republican regulars were loyal to Nixon and wary of Rockefeller's liberal tendencies.

Nixon received the nomination on the second ballot. A first-ballot victory was thwarted by adherents of the conservative senator from Arizona, Barry Goldwater, whose denunciations of the New Deal legacy were far more vehement than those of most Republicans. Nixon prevailed, though Rockefeller's strength was sufficient to prompt an extraordinary conference in New York before the convention, in which Nixon agreed to a series of liberal planks to the Republican platform.

The election centered on issues of cold war confrontation with the Soviet Union and its allies. The collapse of a summit conference because of a U-2 reconnaissance flight over Russia and the recent "loss" of Cuba to Communism quickened the debate over which of the parties was better suited to the challenge of the '60s. On the whole, as pollsters have agreed, Kennedy projected the stronger, more confident image. Nixon exhausted himself in an ill-advised pledge to campaign in all 50 states. Perhaps because the genial leadership of Eisenhower constituted a difficult act to follow, or perhaps because of his own brooding personality, Nixon exuded tension. In his famous televised debates with Kennedy, he seemed too frequently defensive. Moreover, the strength of Eisenhower's presence was not employed in the Nixon campaign until near the election itself.

In one of the closest elections in American history, Senator Kennedy won. While the electoral vote was 303 to 219, a shift of a few thousand votes in the major cities would have made the Republicans victorious. The Democratic South was an important factor, but the urban vote was decisive. Though returns from Chicago showed possible irregularities, Nixon decided not to press the issue.

However narrow his victory in 1960, Kennedy became a popular President. His program, the New Frontier, instilled a sense of national service and adventure. Kennedy's eloquent oratorical style was leavened with engaging humor and wit. Through the Peace Corps and the space program he peacefully challenged the Russians while taking the lead in domestic reforms such as Medicare and civil rights. The civil rights movement was steadily growing, and a huge march on Washington in 1963 built support for sweeping legislation to enforce the guarantees of the Radical Republicans' 14th Amendment.

With Republican support, Kennedy moved from early confrontations with Russia—the abortive ''Bay of Pigs'' invasion of Cuba in 1961 and the 1962 crisis over Russian missiles in that country—to the vision of détente hinted at in the Nuclear Test Ban Treaty of 1963. But through it all, Kennedy maintained a commitment to confront communist subversion in the Third World through counterinsurgency programs. This commitment leaves a question regarding what might have happened to Kennedy's political career, given the subsequent developments in Vietnam.

The Democratic victory of 1960 polarized the Republican Party. When Nixon was defeated in a bid for the California governorship in 1962, moderate Republicans were caught in a war between two ideological factions. On the one side were liberal Republicans such as Nelson Rockefeller, Hugh Scott, and Jacob Javits—men whose support for a socially active role for government continued the tradition of Justin Morrill, Theodore Roosevelt, and the policies of Willkie and Dewey. On the other side were conservatives such as Barry

A new tonic for conservatives, a can of ''Gold Water'' symbolizes the 1964 presidential candidacy of Senator Barry Goldwater of Arizona. Four years earlier, Richard M. Nixon had lost a close race to John F. Kennedy, and the Republican Party was polarized into two ideological factions. One side consisted of liberal Republicans, such as Nelson Rockefeller, who advocated a strong government hand in social issues. To promote their progressive ideals, the moderate Republicans formed the Ripon Society in 1962. On the other side stood conservatives such as Barry Goldwater, leaders committed to the laissez-faire principles espoused by Calvin Coolidge. Crippled by their divided ranks, the Republicans suffered a devastating loss at the polls in 1964. The Democrats, with Lyndon Baines Johnson and his promise of a Great Society, captured 486 electoral votes, the largest majority yet recorded in American history.

Goldwater, leaders committed to the principle of laissez-faire that can be traced back from Calvin Coolidge to Jackson and Jefferson. In 1962, moderate Republicans formed the Ripon Society to promote their progressive ideals.

The shocking murder of President Kennedy in 1963 left various reform proposals in the hands of the new President, Lyndon Baines Johnson. Johnson, the former Senate majority leader, aspired to be a President of Franklin Roosevelt's stature. The central goal of his program, dubbed the Great Society, was a war on poverty. Johnson's program entailed such extensions of the welfare state that the ideological division of Republicans was sharpened.

Since Johnson was clearly destined to be the Democratic nominee in 1964, debates among Republicans centered on how to respond to the President's social vision. Already, his legislative skill (and the sorrow caused by Kennedy's death) had prompted passage of the Civil Rights Act of 1964. But Johnson intended much more than this, and the response of the Goldwater faction was one of alarm. Goldwater—with the backing of ultraconservative groups such as the John Birch Society—sought to confront the whole concept of government activism, which many of his supporters called "creeping socialism."

Though Nixon was defeated in his gubernatorial bid in 1962, Rockefeller easily won reelection, and liberal-to-moderate Republicans George Romney and William Scranton were elected to the governorships of Michigan and Pennsylvania. All these men were considered prime presidential prospects in 1964, but the leadership of the party's liberal wing passed to Rockefeller, who proceeded to spar with Goldwater in the presidential primaries.

Slowly but relentlessly, Goldwater built up delegate support, and when he won the California primary on June 2, the nomination was all but his. Liberals and moderates reacted with alarm. On June 12, Governor Scranton announced a last-minute candidacy to stop Goldwater. This only served to divide the party further. Goldwater was nominated on the first ballot. His running mate was Representative William Miller of New York.

The Republican Convention of 1964, held in San Francisco, was one of the most tumultuous in the party's history. Goldwater's forces had virtually complete supremacy, and proposed platform planks denouncing extremist organizations were defeated. Governor Rockefeller, speaking on behalf of the proposed antiextremist planks, was booed by the Goldwater delegates. Goldwater himself, in his acceptance speech, declared that "extremism in the defense of liberty is no vice," and that "moderation in the pursuit of justice is no virtue."

The Democrats, as expected, nominated LBJ; his running mate was the liberal Minnesota senator, Hubert Humphrey. In their campaign, the Democrats emphasized the legacy of John F. Kennedy and urged the adoption of Johnson's proposed Great Society programs. The tone of the Democratic campaign was described at the time as one of euphoria, largely because the press was overwhelmingly negative toward the Goldwater candidacy, and the polls showed Johnson firmly in the lead. The election was the greatest landslide yet to occur in American history: The electoral vote was 486 for Johnson, 52 for Goldwater.

This devastating Republican defeat would for a time reduce the influence of conservative Republicans. But the Democrats, temporarily victorious and strengthened by congressional majorities, were soon to have traumas of their own. For in 1965, at the urging of members of his Cabinet and foreign policy advisors, Johnson began an escalation of the American involvement in Vietnam in an effort to decisively defeat the communist insurgency there. Thus began one of the longest, most agonizing wars in American history.

Johnson hoped for a quick military victory, so as not to disrupt his plans for the Great Society. But the war became a quagmire, and even members of the Democratic Party questioned its premises. Many critics believed the war was unwinnable short of a nuclear strike. Others believed that the tactics of "search and

In Vietnam, President Richard M. Nixon boosts the morale of American combat men in 1969. During his first term as the 37th President, Nixon endeavored to reconcile a nation painfully torn by turbulence in the cities and a long, agonizing war overseas. He succeeded in ending American fighting in Vietnam. In his second term, however, Nixon's involvement with the Watergate scandal brought fresh divisions to the country. His participation in an attempted cover-up of the burglary of the Democratic National Headquarters in Washington, D.C., forced him to become the first U.S. President to resign from office.

destroy," which were aimed at the communist Vietcong, would devastate the entire countryside and populace of Vietnam.

The war proved disastrous for Johnson, and it triggered fundamental changes in American culture. Significant numbers of young Americans rebelled at the prospect of serving in Vietnam. Many sought refuge in a counterculture based upon psychedelic drugs and quasi-religious cults. Urban blacks, impatient with the pace of reform, sought economic gains commensurate with recent advances in civil rights. In what sociologists call the "revolution of rising expectations," a movement for "black power" developed. Annual summer riots in urban ghettoes, riots to protest the overwhelming poverty of urban blacks, bred a climate of fear among the white middle class. Added to this was the growing "generation gap" that separated younger and older Americans.

Some of these issues affected the outcome of the 1966 midterm elections, in which a backlash against liberal policies thinned Democratic majorities in Congress. But the real effects were felt in the extraordinary presidential election of 1968. President Johnson was challenged in his own party by the maverick candidacy of Senator Eugene McCarthy of Minnesota, and later by Senator Robert Kennedy, the younger brother of the murdered President. Two stunning developments added to the Democratic turmoil: the decision by President Johnson not to seek reelection and the horrid murder of Senator Kennedy, five years after his brother's assassination. Vice President Hubert Humphrey and Senator McCarthy continued the struggle to the cataclysmic Democratic convention in Chicago, which was marred by street riots and police brutality. Humphrey was the luckless nominee. A further complication to the 1968 election was the third-party candidacy of Alabama Governor George Wallace on a platform of law and order.

The aspiring Republican candidates in 1968 included George Romney, Richard Nixon, Governor Ronald Reagan of California (a Goldwater-backer in 1964), John V. Lindsay, the liberal mayor of New York, and liberal-to-moderate Senators Charles Percy of Illinois and Mark Hatfield of Oregon. Rockefeller denied presidential ambitions until the eleventh hour, at which point Richard Nixon, at the height of a spectacular comeback, clinched the nomination. His running mate was the little-known governor of Maryland, Spiro T. Agnew.

The election of 1968 was yet another close contest, from which the Republicans emerged victorious. At last, Richard Nixon, who had labored so long in the shadow of Dwight D. Eisenhower, had a chance to prove himself. The "New Nixon," as the media dubbed him, assumed the Presidency in one of America's most divisive periods. His campaign had pledged tougher law and order policies directed at "crime in the streets." But he also pledged to "bring us together," to heal the social divisions afflicting the country.

Nixon's first six months in office were quiet. However, by fall of 1969, confrontations over American involvement in Vietnam began to burst forth anew. Major protests were held in October and November in Washington. The new Vice President, Spiro Agnew, castigated the protesters as "nattering nabobs of negativism" and "effete impudent snobs." The President appealed to a "silent majority" of American citizens, those he believed unwilling to see a sudden end to the war in Vietnam at the expense of America's honor.

By the spring of 1970, the polarization had worsened as Nixon extended the war zone to Cambodia. Blood was shed on the campus of Kent State University in Ohio when students protesting the war clashed with the National Guard. The stern image of the Nixon policies was constantly sharpened by the rhetoric of Vice President Agnew and Attorney General John Mitchell. In addition, J. Edgar Hoover, the aging director of the Federal Bureau of Investigation, was given considerable leeway in his efforts to investigate alleged subversion.

In contrast, it seemed, to the antigovernment stance of Goldwater in '64, the Nixon

Administration sought refuge in the power of the state and defended the establishment at every turn. And yet, the Nixon years were more complex than this suggests. Though he and Vice President Agnew defended the various police powers of the central government, Nixon embraced a program of revenue-sharing to bring about a "new federalism," a return of power to the states. While he fought to maintain his own schedule for "peace with honor" in Vietnam, Nixon, along with National Security Advisor Henry Kissinger, took steps that would lead to a remarkable reconciliation with Red China in 1972. Largely under the influence of Special Advisor Daniel P. Moynihan, Nixon proposed a plan of welfare reform that would establish a minimum guaranteed income for poor families. And, to deal with growing inflation, Nixon was willing to experiment briefly with limited wage and price controls.

But throughout the first Nixon Administration, the confrontations proceeded. As part of the so-called "southern strategy" crafted by Republican theorist Kevin Phillips and others, Nixon attempted to nominate southern jurists to Supreme Court vacancies, in part to steal the thunder of Alabama's George Wallace. Two southern nominees in a row, Clement Haynesworth and G. Harrold Carswell, were rejected by the Senate. Nixon's reaction was combative.

In the 1970 congressional elections, Nixon and Agnew openly sought to purge liberal Republicans, men such as Senator Charles Goodell, whom Agnew referred to as "Radiclibs." This drew the protest of Nixon's Interior Secretary, Walter Hickel. But the Agnew attacks went on, and Hickel departed the administration. With the exception of the respect he accorded Henry Kissinger, Nixon came to depend less on his Cabinet or congressional leaders than on a loyal group of White House staff members, an entourage headed by the "palace guards," John Ehrlichman and H.R. Haldeman.

In the election of 1972, Nixon made the most of incumbency. His slogan was "Four

Diplomatic masterstroke: President Nixon meets with Chou En-lai, leader of Red China, in 1972. Nixon's surprise "journey of peace" to China reduced tensions with that country and with the Soviet Union. During his tenure, Nixon made other notable strides in foreign policy. His summit meetings with Soviet leader Leonid I. Brezhnev yielded a treaty to limit strategic nuclear weapons. In 1974, Nixon's Secretary of State, Henry Kissinger, negotiated disengagement agreements in the conflict between Israel and its adversaries, Egypt and Syria. On the domestic front, Nixon's achievements included revenue sharing, the end of the draft, new anticrime laws, and a broad environmental program.

More Years," and the campaign was entrusted to a special Committee to Re-Elect the President. The Democrats were divided by the rival candidacies of Hubert Humphrey and Senators Edmund Muskie of Maine, Henry Jackson of Washington, and George McGovern of South Dakota. McGovern, who managed to unite the forces that had volunteered to work for McCarthy and Kennedy in '68, was the front-runner, and the last-minute effort by Humphrey to block the nomination was futile. McGovern's campaign, largely based on opposition to the war in Vietnam, was set back by a change in running mates. His first selection, Senator Thomas Eagleton of Missouri, belatedly revealed a history of psychiatric treatment. Senator Eagleton's replacement was Sargent Shriver, the former director of the Peace Corps.

The election was an overwhelming landslide victory for Nixon and Agnew. The electoral vote was 520 to 17. In part, McGovern suffered from the image of "extremism" that had marred Barry Goldwater's candidacy in 1964—though the two were at opposite ends of the political spectrum. But in all probability, most Americans also agreed in 1972 that Nixon's leadership was more attuned to the needs of the country than was McGovern's. In the flush of victory, Nixon prepared for new confrontations over impoundments of congressionally appropriated funds, executive privilege, and further extensions of presidential prerogative. But for Richard Nixon, events were soon to escape control.

An Age of Repudiations: 1972 to the Present

In February 1972, President Nixon traveled to Peking to meet with Chinese leaders Chou En-lai and Mao Tse-tung. This would have been literally unbelievable a few years earlier. Only a Republican leader whose anticommunist credentials were above reproach could have engineered such a diplomatic masterstroke, said Senator Mike Mansfield. The initiative for the meeting came from Red China itself, for the Peking leadership was anxious to bury its differences with America, largely out of fear of the Soviet Union. National Security Advisor Henry Kissinger urged the President to consider the initiative favorably. Nixon, to his great credit, took the advice and thus altered the balance of power and opened new opportunities for world peace.

A few months later, however, on June 16, 1972, five men were arrested at the headquarters suite of the Democratic National Committee in the huge Watergate Hotel complex in Washington. Though the men were linked to the Committee to Re-Elect the President, George McGovern failed in his efforts to make a major campaign issue out of the break-in. The Watergate affair, however, was to be the undoing of the Nixon Presidency within two years. Watergate constituted a major national tragedy. It also revealed that the combative streak in Nixon's leadership sprang from a fundamental lack of appreciation for American traditions and history.

Early in 1973, James McCord, one of the Watergate burglars, revealed in his trial before Judge John Sirica—a Republican jurist—that responsibility for the break-in could be traced to the White House. In April, presidential counsels John Dean and Jeb Stuart Magruder confirmed and expanded the charges, leading to the resignations of Attorney General Mitchell, H.R. Haldeman, and John Ehrlichman, as well as to the appointment of a special prosecutor by President Nixon.

Congressional hearings in the summer of 1973, under the chairmanship of Senator Sam Ervin, revealed that White House reprisals had been directed at an "enemies list"—political opponents targeted for special, illegal harassment. The hearings also revealed that hush money had been paid to the Watergate burglars to keep them silent, and that tape recordings of White House conversations existed that could possibly confirm allegations against the President and his staff. A long struggle ensued to obtain the tape recordings, a struggle featuring claims of executive privi-

lege in withholding possible evidence. The fight over the tapes resulted in the firing of special prosecutor Archibald Cox in October 1973. Soon afterward, congressional leaders took steps to initiate impeachment proceedings against President Nixon.

At this point, Watergate completely dominated national politics. Vietnam was no longer a major issue, since American involvement had virtually ended early in 1973. As a sidelight to Watergate, Spiro Agnew was forced to resign the vice presidency in October 1973 due to allegations of corruption and bribery while he was governor of Maryland. Under the terms of the recently adopted 25th Amendment to the Constitution, President Nixon nominated Representative Gerald Ford of Michigan to succeed Agnew, and on December 6, 1973, Ford took the vice presidential oath of office.

Watergate was finally resolved in 1974 when the long struggle for the White House tape recordings ended. Both the House Judiciary Committee, investigating articles of impeachment, and the new special prosecutor,

Taking the oath of office from Chief Justice Warren Burger on August 9, 1974, Gerald R. Ford ascends from the vice presidency to the office Richard Nixon gave up to avoid impeachment. Earlier, Ford had taken over as Vice President from Spiro Agnew, who was forced to resign due to allegations of corruption and bribery while he was governor of Maryland. Ford became the first U.S. Vice President chosen under the terms of the 25th Amendment. When he took the presidential oath, Ford noted the unprecedented times: "I assume the Presidency under extraordinary circumstances. . . . This is the hour of history that troubles our minds and hurts our hearts." To help heal the nation and free the process of government from the paralysis of Watergate investigations, Ford granted Nixon an unconditional pardon. During his administration, Ford coped with Herculean challenges—curbing inflation, reviving a depressed economy, solving chronic energy shortages, and trying to ensure world peace.

Leon Jaworski, demanded the tapes. In July, the Supreme Court ruled that they had to be released. The tapes—especially a June 4, 1972, recording—clearly implicated Nixon in the Watergate cover-up. In late July, the Judiciary Committee voted three articles of impeachment. Nixon, facing almost certain impeachment by the full House, resigned on August 8, and Gerald Ford was sworn in as the nation's 38th President.

In the wake of the Watergate disaster, the Republican Party had a President in Gerald Ford who epitomized the same virtues of decency and simplicity possessed by Dwight Eisenhower. Ford, the former minority leader in the House, had established a conservative-to-moderate record. Upon taking the presidential oath, he announced to the country that the "long nightmare" of Watergate was ended and a process of healing had begun. He retained almost all the Nixon Cabinet, especially Henry Kissinger as Secretary of State. Ford nominated Nelson Rockefeller as his own Vice President under the terms of the 25th Amendment.

Ford's first controversial act was the extension of a personal presidential pardon to Richard Nixon, thus preventing any further criminal prosecution of the former President. The decision to extend the pardon, though prompted by compassion and the broader interests of the country, was not universally popular. President Ford, moreover, was bedeviled by the twin economic problems of inflation and recession, along with a severe escalation in the price of oil by OPEC, the international cartel.

None of these problems by itself was fatal, but each demanded action. Yet while the public wanted action, it cast a suspicious eye on the White House in the aftermath of Vietnam and Watergate. A major theme in the coming election of 1976 was a desire to repudiate the recent past and to blame its evils on excessive power in Washington. Though Ford was profoundly different from Nixon, his pardon of the former President continued to link the two in the minds of many voters.

Two "outsiders" to Washington benefited most directly from the mood to repudiate the Nixon legacy: former Governor Ronald Reagan of California and Governor Jimmy Carter of Georgia. Reagan challenged Ford for the Republican nomination and came very close to an upset convention victory. Ford prevailed, but the power of Reagan and his following forced Ford into more conservative positions on social issues and a tougher stance on defense spending. To further appease Reagan and his following, Ford selected a conservative running mate, Senator Robert Dole of Kansas.

Jimmy Carter had eliminated his chief Democratic opponents—Senator Henry Jackson, Representative Morris Udall, and Governor George Wallace—in the spring primaries, and he was easily nominated on the first ballot. As a Southerner committed to civil rights, Carter appeared to embody the spirit of reconciliation, and his platform style, with its sweet-natured delivery, symbolized this. He promised Americans "a government as good as its people," thus setting the tone for post-Watergate politics.

The 1976 campaign was undistinguished in the extreme. Carter's general vagueness almost lost him the election, but there were several mistakes in the Ford camp as well. The candidates met in a series of televised debates. However, the debates did not measure up to the quality that might have been expected. Carter was elected by an electoral college vote of 297 to 241.

Carter's first symbolic act was to walk down Pennsylvania Avenue on Inauguration Day, thus signalling a more open Presidency. His record was mixed. An outstanding success in foreign policy, the 1978 Camp David accords between Israel and Egypt, seemed to offer hope for an eventual peace in the strife-torn Middle East. Carter's emphasis on human rights, though more controversial, helped America's image abroad. But his post-Watergate emphasis on reconciliation seemed, at times, to preclude presidential firmness. The President's campaign advantage of 1976—

Early-day champion of women's rights, the Republican Party counts among its ranks many notable women leaders. Among the current luminaries are: Elizabeth Hanford Dole, former Secretary of Transportation (upper left); Sandra Day O'Connor, Associate Justice of the U.S. Supreme Court (upper right); Constance Morella, Congresswoman from the Eighth District of Maryland (lower left); and Jeanne Kirkpatrick, political scientist, columnist, and former U.S. representative to the United Nations (lower right).

his position as a Washington "outsider"—became a handicap in congressional relations and in executive branch administration. In both areas, Carter and his White House staff were inept.

Carter, like Ford, was beset by the energy crisis. Many viewed the dependence on foreign oil as a symptom of long-term strategic weakness in a world of diminishing energy supplies. In the short-term, however, the energy crisis was the result of the defiant OPEC cartel's pricing policies. To deal with OPEC, Carter proposed a series of belt-tightening measures to save energy. While almost universally lauded at the time, these measures bred hidden resentment. This resentment was compounded in 1979 when militant Iranians, their country in the throes of an Islamic revolution, seized American diplomats and held them hostage.

The question of the 1980 election increasingly hinged upon the fate of the hostages. The crisis proved to be Carter's undoing, just as the Watergate affair had been Nixon's. For over a year, the American diplomats were held and tortured with the approval of the Iranian government. Negotiations led nowhere, and an ill-fated military rescue attempt in April 1980 only increased Americans' sense of humiliation and impotence. Moreover, a Soviet invasion of Afghanistan in December 1979—though it prompted a sudden anti-Soviet shift in Carter's foreign policy—added to the growing malaise.

Carter's weakness prompted challenges in 1980 from Governor Edmund Brown of California and Senator Edward Kennedy of Massachusetts. Kennedy, the last surviving brother of the murdered President, was a forceful liberal orator whose record, however, was tarnished by mysteries surrounding a 1969 automobile accident at Chappaquiddick, Massachusetts. Kennedy did not succeed in capturing the Democratic nomination from Carter, but his challenge severely crippled the party's chances in the national election.

The Republican front-runner was Ronald Reagan, the conservatives' champion. After turning aside an early challenge from John Connally, a conservative Nixon-era convert from the Democratic Party, Reagan swept to victory. He appealed to the same constituency as did Goldwater in 1964—those conservatives who wished to reverse the flow of power to the central government begun in the days of FDR. Reagan also appealed to religious fundamentalists, especially the so-called Moral Majority, who looked with disfavor upon the permissiveness spawned by the 1960s and '70s. But most of all—and unlike Goldwater—Reagan appealed to a broad spectrum of American voters as an easygoing and reassuring leader. His style was also a contrast to Carter's inarticulate vagueness. Reagan's running mate was moderate George Bush.

There is legitimate question as to whether the Reagan victory in 1980 reflected a repudiation of Carter or an acceptance of Reagan. In many ways, 1980, like 1976, was a year of repudiation. In 1976 the voters had been anxious to repudiate the Nixon "imperial Presidency." In 1980, they were equally anxious to repudiate Carter's perceived weakness.

The 1980 election was a three-way race. Maverick liberal Republican Representative John Anderson ran as an independent, contending that neither Carter nor Reagan had an adequate agenda for America's social problems. In a series of televised debates, the candidates faced each other in groups of two: Reagan and Anderson, Carter and Anderson, Carter and Reagan. The final debate between Carter and Reagan was decisive, according to the pollsters. Reagan's sincerity and firmness contrasted sharply with Carter's desperation, leading to an emotional tidal wave at the polls. The electoral college victory for Reagan was 489 to 49.

The Reagan years began auspiciously enough, since on Inauguration Day the Iranians freed the hostages. Instead of punishing Iran, Reagan urged Americans to turn their thoughts from vengeance. On his 70th day in office, the President showed heroic qualities when struck by a madman's bullet, from which he quickly recovered.

Reagan, a former Hollywood star and a convert from New Deal liberalism, was firmly convinced that America's social and economic problems universally stemmed from excessive government. He and his followers believed the only true conservatism was the creed of laissez-faire. In particular, Reagan embraced an updated variation of laissez-faire called "supply-side" economics, touted by writers such as George Gilder and congressional leaders such as Representative Jack Kemp of New York. Supply-side economics placed no emphasis on government programs to further job training or industrial productivity. Rather it

"The Great Communicator," President Ronald Reagan—a former Hollywood actor—addresses the nation during a weekly radio broadcast. His relaxed conversational tone and reassuring manner touched a responsive chord with voters eager to repudiate the "imperial Presidency" of Nixon and the inarticulate vagueness of Jimmy Carter. During his first term, Reagan brought about a strong business recovery, improved employment, and achieved a renewal of national self-confidence. These successes and his widespread personal popularity won him a second term in 1984 with the largest landslide victory in history.

relied on tax incentives to spur industry to further efforts of its own. This policy, combined with related cuts in nonmilitary expenditures and huge increases in defense spending, led to budget battles in Congress. Reagan, his power bolstered by Republican control of the Senate and increased power in the House, carried the day in the congressional battles of 1981. His budget director, David Stockman, became a central figure in the battle.

However, by the winter of 1981-82, the political outlook shifted. While Reagan's austerity, together with a policy of tight money at the Federal Reserve, significantly cut inflation, the nation fell into a deep recession, with rising unemployment. The huge increases in defense spending and the decreasing government revenues bred tremendous budget deficits. Federal borrowing threatened to compete with the borrowing needs of the private sector and thus keep interest rates high. Economic fears were increased by revelations from David Stockman that administration budget projections had been faulty. Other voices began to be heard in the party. One Republican moderate, Representative Jim Leach of Iowa—newly elected chairman of the Ripon Society and leader of the so-called "Gypsy Moth" faction of Republican moderates—issued a "moderate manifesto" in September 1981 challenging the views prevailing in Republican leadership circles.

The recession led to Democratic gains in the 1982 congressional elections. But despite the problem of rising deficits, a strong economic recovery, along with the widespread personal popularity of the President, led to a landslide victory for Reagan in 1984. The President defeated Democratic challenger Walter Mondale by an electoral vote of 525 to 13. However, the wide margin of Reagan's win failed to substantially alter the balance of power in Congress. The Republican Senate majority was actually reduced by two, while in the House the Democrats retained their slight majority.

President Reagan's second term has been highlighted by real accomplishments, such as the continued economic recovery and the rising prospect of international arms control agreements. But the latter years of the Reagan Presidency have been indelibly marked by the Iran-contra affair. This book goes to press just as the Iran-contra congressional hearings conclude. It is too soon for a historical analysis of this episode. It will take time and reflection to evaluate just what the hearings' disclosures mean for the Republican Party and its future.

Nevertheless, as we look to the future, we can rest assured that the Republican Party will remain strong and vital, a thriving and developing institution that answers to a host of abiding dreams, principles, and challenges. Its triumphs endure, yet the Republican Party continues to struggle with defining its principles, as philosophically derived institutions should always struggle. Its challenge is the basic problem of determining which of its contrasting outlooks, laissez-faire or noblesse oblige, is best suited to the times. In answering this challenge lies the adventure, and the ultimate distinction, of being a Republican.

Tempered by humbling defeats and buoyed by dazzling triumphs, the Grand Old Party stands strong after 130 years of challenge. In its coming of age, the party has helped preserve and mold a union of states where future generations can benefit from the American experience. Rule by the people—a principle unbowed by the strife of a thousand political battles—guides Republicans as they prepare for the tasks of tomorrow. It is from this idea of government—a republic—that the Grand Old Party continues to draw its strength.

My 60 Years As A Republican:
Some Observations and Conclusions

Many times over the years several of my colleagues have asked me to set down my thoughts on the Republican Party. When shown the early drafts of this work, they invariably requested that it conclude with a personal testament of my political philosophy. I now do so with both pride and reluctance—with pride because political moderation is my heartfelt conviction—and with reluctance because it is not my intention to convert anyone from their equally heartfelt convictions.

The Republican Party is a remarkable institution, as vast and varied as our great nation. The diversity within our party is its strength, just as the diversity within our nation gives it vitality and purpose. This conclusion is warranted when one looks back upon Republican history. Think of the diversity that has existed within the party—the Radical Republicans of Lincoln's day and the Progressives of Teddy Roosevelt's era just to name two. Totalitarian regimes stagnate from rigidly imposed ideologies which stifle freedom of thought; our form of government profits from the free exchange of differences of opinion.

This book is the result of my 60 years' experience as a Republican. As the party of Lincoln, the party of Teddy Roosevelt, the party of Herbert Hoover, and the party of my father, the Republican Party has been and always will be the party of my heritage. The current generation's ignorance of their heritage and history is a cause for alarm to concerned Republicans such as you and I. We must never forget that our heritage must be transmitted; that it must be learned and earned by each succeeding generation. The first purpose of this book, therefore, is to capture the heritage of the Republican Party in an easily accessible form.

I am a Republican in one sense because my father was a Republican. Five years after my father immigrated to Iowa from Germany he became an American citizen. One of my fondest childhood memories is of how thrilled he was when soon thereafter he was elected to the local township school board. Although he always claimed to be an independent voter, he invariably voted for Republican candidates

because, he said, "The Republicans always have the best candidates." My father consistently encouraged me to be an active citizen, and I believe that this helps explain why I developed a lifelong interest in politics and in the Republican Party.

"Education," Will and Ariel Durant have observed, "is the transmission of civilization." I endorse this conclusion, and my own education consolidated my Republicanism. As a college student in the late 1920s at the then North East Missouri State Teachers College (now Northeast Missouri State University), I was influenced by one of my political science teachers, Dr. Willis McClure, to become involved in both college and national politics. Dr. McClure was a Republican, but he encouraged me to attend the political rallies for both Democratic candidate Al Smith and Republican candidate Herbert Hoover in 1928. As a result, I became an active Republican, first in the Hoover campaigns of 1928 and 1932 and later in Alf Landon's 1936 campaign.

It has now been a half-century since those early experiences. My Republican philosophy, tempered in the crucible of public service, has matured over those 50 years. I now proudly consider myself a moderate Republican. It is my firm belief that the past greatness and the future success of the party rest in the principle of moderation. Thus the second and larger purpose of this book is to challenge Republicans to reexamine their own heritage and to unite behind the party's traditional commitment to moderation and fiscal responsibility.

Thanks to the influence and urging of Charles Wittenmeyer of Davenport, with whom I labored to make Scott County Republican again, I was elected to the Iowa Legislature in 1944 and to the United States Congress in 1954. That made it possible for me to influence and to help direct Republican policy.

I did not become fully aware of my moderate Republicanism until the 1964 presidential campaign compelled me, like many other Americans, to define my own political philosophy. I instinctively disagreed when Barry Goldwater stated: "I would remind you that extremism in the defense of liberty is no vice: and let me remind you also that moderation in the pursuit of justice is no virtue." Senator Goldwater's motivation was sincere, as his outstanding subsequent career has demonstrated, but his choice of words was most unfortunate.

Moderation A Virtue

I believe that moderation *is* a virtue—especially in a democracy of contending interests—and that extremism is a divisive vice. My reaction in 1964 led me to conduct research on political moderation. I have come to the conclusion that moderation is to be recommended above all political philosophies because it alone recognizes the common fate and aspirations of all human beings; it alone understands the influences that drive people to extremes; and, finally, moderation alone respects the sacredness of humanity. Moreover, I have discovered that the Republican Party has a heritage of moderation. Lincoln, far from being the radical, was a moderate who followed Ben Franklin's advice to "avoid extremes." As Lincoln stated in 1856:

"In grave emergencies moderation is generally safer than radicalism. . . . As it now stands we must appeal to the sober sense and patriotism of the people. We will make converts day by day; we will grow stronger by calmness and moderation; we will grow strong by the violence and injustice of our adversaries; and unless truth be a mockery and justice a hollow lie we will be in the majority after a while and then the revolution which we will accomplish will be none the less radical from being the result of pacific measures."

These are words for our party to ponder and to live by. Especially is this true in this bicentennial period, when we commemorate the establishment of our republic and our republican form of government. The Constitution itself was drafted to create a balanced government. Moderation and balance charac-terized the philosophy of the Constitution and its principal architect, James Madison. In No. 37 of *The Federalist*, Madison moaned: "It is a misfortune, inseparable from human affairs, that public measures are rarely investigated with that spirit of moderation which is essential to a just estimate of their real tendency to advance or obstruct the public good." The separation of powers and the checks and balances built into the constitutional system were designed to prevent the immoderate use of power by any individuals or factions.

During my early years in the Iowa Legislature I developed the reputation of being somewhat of an independent because of my moderate Republican philosophy. I can still vividly recall how upset the party leaders were when I led the successful fight for state funding of public education in the Iowa Legislature. The party which created the land-grant college system, I believed, and still believe, had a unique commitment to support and to encourage public education. It still irritates me when some Republicans, Democrats, and Independents question the wisdom of spending money on education. I've always claimed that money appropriated for education is not money spent, it is money invested in our future. The people of the United States have never made a more rewarding investment.

My strong commitment to the principles of the party of Lincoln motivated my leadership in the movement in Iowa for the principle of one man-one vote. Seventeen years later the Supreme Court of the United States handed down the decision making that philosophy mandatory. Today most Republicans in Iowa rightly take pride for their pioneering role in implementing the one man-one vote philosophy and for their support of public schools by initiating state investment in education.

My moderate Republicanism has always been predicated on the pragmatic and caring approach. In a democracy we must govern ourselves with compassion for all of our fellow citizens as well as for generations to come. This approach has characterized the moderate position on federal investment in worthy programs. I have never opposed investing in programs where the need was clear and evident, but I have always insisted that such programs include a reasonable and sound system of financing. I was one of the legislative leaders who helped persuade President Eisenhower to provide such a plan to pay for the Interstate Highway System as it was built. To finance programs on borrowed money is the height of irresponsible government. It visits the sins of the present on future generations. We need to remember the wise advice of Seneca, "It is the quality of a great soul . . . to prefer moderation to excess."

The Republican Party has traditionally supported individual rights and defended the Constitution. In my career, I have consistently opposed those both in and out of my party who would tamper with the constitutional separation of church and state through the so-called prayer amendment. Our constitutionally guaranteed religious liberties allow for the fullest free development of religion. For government to intervene in religious matters would be for it to interfere with individuals' freedoms. The American concept of the separation of church and state has benefited religion more than have the doctrines claimed by any other nation.

During my career I identified with other Republican moderates such as Eisenhower, Walter Judd, Gerald Ford, and William Scranton. In recent years I have been disturbed by the tendency of some within the party to abandon the party's heritage of moderation for more dogmatic political ideologies. "Moderation," as the ancient philosopher Euripides wrote, is "the noblest gift of heaven." I am heartened, therefore, by a resurgence among Republican moderates, which has received its best statement from a prominent Republican who concluded that it is moderate Republicanism "which is the repository of the mainstream of Republican tradition."

As the party faces the challenges of the present and looks ahead to the future, we must ensure that the essential decency and honesty of the American people prevail over the selfish interests of those wedded to dogmatic ideologies. Moderate Republicanism best meets that need both for our party and for our nation. As a moderate, I offer the following seven points to guide our policies.

Suggested Party Guidelines

1) A responsible foreign policy which rejects unilateral interventionism, leads the effort to control and reduce the arms race, and strives to strengthen international institutions such as the United Nations;

2) a renewal of the Republican commitment to education in order to prepare coming generations to meet responsibilities greater than any ever faced;

3) a sound plan for fiscal responsibility to control both the size of the budget and to conquer inflation so that American families may continue to prosper;

4) a realization that technological innovation must be moderated by our responsibility to retrain displaced workers;

5) a farm policy which promotes the prosperity and security of American farmers, accompanied by a positive and responsible conservation policy based on the realization that the only perpetual natural resource we have is the earth's soil;

6) a renewed commitment to the constitutional separation of church and state, with an understanding that the best impact government and political leaders can have upon American moral standards is for them to convey the highest ethical standards in their actions;

7) and, in the party's tradition of Lincoln and emancipation, a commitment to continue and intensify our efforts to provide equality of opportunity regardless of race, creed, or sex.

Today the Republican Party faces problems as contentious and ominous as those it faced in the 1850s. Decades of unrestrained government spending have created a national debt of unthinkable proportions. Lee Iacocca estimated in 1986 that it would take the U.S. Mint 57 years, two months, and two weeks just to print the bills to pay off the current debt. Is this to be our legacy to future generations? We have addressed the social ills of the 20th century—drugs, crime, urban decay, poverty, pornography, and the divisive debate over abortion—with slogans and the outworn ideological demagoguery of the Right and the Left. Why has this been so? I believe that it is because our leaders have forgotten American history. Not since Presidents Kennedy and Eisenhower have we had a President with a sense of history. Too often our leaders have not only known nothing of our history, but some have also been uninterested, even contemptuous, of it. Only if we can free ourselves from "the terrorists of the mind," to use A. Bartlett Giamatti's phrase, can we return to the true principles of moderation.

How then does the Reagan Administration's record comport with the historical principles of moderate Republicanism? It must be noted that Reagan has moved, at times hesitantly, to a more moderate position. His recommendation to reform the tax system once his initial tax cut proved ill-advised is indicative of that moderation. Evaluated from the vantage point of history, the President's economic policies to date have not displayed any systematic commitment to moderate principles. Opposition from Congress has played an important role, though Reagan has given no evidence of having had, as Mondale and the Democrats alleged, a secret plan or a hidden agenda with which to address the nation's fiscal crisis. But it is just such a well-thought-out plan, based upon moderate Republican principles of fiscal responsibility and balanced budgets, as well as social responsibility, that the party must develop to meet current and future challenges.

To those who fault the President, it must be noted that Reagan has reenergized the Presidency. Indeed his leadership has had a moderating influence in some important areas of our society. His handling of the air traffic controllers' strike, his insistence on salvaging Social Security, and his firm support of free trade are among the outstanding evidences of his leadership. The President's advocacy of the line item veto also indicates farsighted leadership. By strenuously supporting the line item veto, the President has paved the way for the eventual adoption of what I believe is an essential means to curb wasteful spending. Probably his most lasting leadership accomplishments have been in foreign affairs—his meeting with Gorbachev in Geneva and his tough stance against terrorism. Although he rejected human rights as a foreign policy determinant, he has subsequently reversed his position and taken a more moderate stance. Those within our party who have criticized the President for exercising moderation and for not implementing some of his earlier rhetoric do not realize that the office has a tempering impact upon its occupant. Just as Reagan has reenergized the office, so too has it moderated his policies and actions.

Of course, the final years of the Reagan Presidency will be judged in light of the revelations of the Iran-contra affair and the publication of the Tower Commission Report. Just as President Reagan was betrayed by some of those whom he trusted in this affair, so too did he fail to exercise the leadership and oversight entrusted to him by the American people. In this his policy was wrong. With commentators proclaiming the end of the Reagan era, and with extremists at both ends of the political spectrum calling for structural changes, it must be asked where we are to go from here as a party. The President himself has shown the way with the selection of Howard Baker for White House Chief of Staff. The Republican Party can weather this crisis only if it hearkens once more to the voice of moderates such as Baker.

It is not my belief that our system needs any major reworking. The Founding Fathers created a system that works, but it is a system that demands public-spirited leaders in and out of government who know the virtue of moderation, not ideologues obsessed with creating their own particular image of the good society without regard for the welfare of the people.

The 18th-century Scottish philosopher and economic theorist Adam Smith wrote that there were two types of leaders. One was the kind of leader "so enamoured with the supposed beauty of his own ideal plan of government" that he comes to believe that he can reorder society much the same "as the hand arranges the different pieces upon a chessboard." The other kind of leader, imbued with a fitting respect for the public good, acts "with proper temper and moderation."

As historian Forrest McDonald has noted, this second kind of leader prevailed in the founding of our nation. George Washington exemplified this kind of inspired and moderate leadership. Washington was a man of character, ever concerned that his actions merit both the trust and the respect of the wise and the virtuous. Much has been written of the Founding Fathers' distrust of human nature and of their desire to create a "system of mutual frustration" to check human imperfections, but it must also be observed that they aspired to create a system which would produce leaders of the stature of Washington. Perhaps we can never return to the level of Washington, but the Republican Party can take the initiative in revitalizing American political leadership. The first step is for Republicans to know their own history.

A number of talented colleagues helped to make this book possible. I cannot conclude without acknowledging my debt of gratitude to them. Thurston B. Morton of Kentucky, while he was National Party Chairman, suggested that I should write a chronicle of Republican achievements because of my interest in history and my experiences in the party. After I had written a detailed outline and much of the original text, I was assisted by five talented researchers and writers: Helen Virden of Mount Pleasant, Iowa; Maier Fox, Richard Striner, and Donald Kennon, all three staff historians of the U. S. Capitol Historical Society; and Richard M. Crum, who produced the picture captions. A special tribute also goes to Joanne Hanson for valuable help in preparing the text. The final text is, of course, my responsibility as its author. The number of political scientists, historians, and party leaders who have read and commented upon the early drafts of this work are too numerous to mention by name, but they all helped to make this a better book. Finally, a professional editor, Paul Martin, and designer, Cynthia Scudder, were engaged to give the book its present form. They have earned my deep-felt appreciation for their efforts.

Together we have created this book. It is certainly not the last word on the Republican Party's heritage and history. Today we face challenges both from within and from without. If the Republican Party can reinvigorate its historical heritage of pragmatism and responsible government, we can face the future with confidence. The Republican Heritage Foundation, of which I am the founding President, is dedicated to transmitting our heritage to present and future generations. We are committed to the study of our party's history and to the dissemination of knowledge concerning our political heritage. This book is but the beginning.

Day by Day Through the History of the Party

JANUARY

1 1863: President Abraham Lincoln signed the Emancipation Proclamation, proclaiming freedom for all persons held as slaves in areas still in rebellion.

2 1900: Secretary of State John Hay announced to the Cabinet the successful negotiation of the Open Door Policy to prevent trade discrimination and preserve China's national identity.

3 1947: The 80th Congress, the first Congress with a Republican majority since 1933, convened. Joseph W. Martin, Jr., was elected Speaker of the House, and Arthur H. Vandenberg was chosen President pro tempore of the Senate.

4 1902: The New Panama Canal Company offered to sell its holdings to the United States for 40 million dollars, prompting the Walker Commission to recommend the Panamanian canal route over the Nicaraguan route.

5 1925: Mrs. Nellie Tayloe Ross was sworn in as governor of Wyoming to succeed her late husband. She was the first woman to serve as governor. She was also the first woman to hold the office of director of the U.S. Mint.

6 1919: Former President Theodore Roosevelt died at his home in Oyster Bay, New York. He was 60 years old.

7 1952: Gen. Dwight D. Eisenhower released a statement in Europe that he was a Republican and that he would not reject an offer to be his party's candidate for President.

8 1867: The Republican-controlled Congress enacted legislation, over the veto of President Andrew Johnson, granting suffrage to blacks in the District of Columbia.

9 1929: The American conscience was quickened when Charles Evans Hughes defended the right of a Socialist elected to the New York State Legislature to serve his term.

10 1878: Senator Aaron Augustus Sargent (R-Calif.) introduced the Women's Suffrage Amendment in the exact wording in which it was ultimately passed.

11 1862: Lincoln accepted Secretary of War Simon P. Cameron's resignation and offered him the post of Minister to Russia.

12 1865: Jefferson Davis, President of the Confederacy, met with an emissary from President Lincoln to discuss peace negotiations.

13 1868: The Republican-controlled Senate refused to accept President Andrew Johnson's ouster of Secretary of War Edwin Stanton. Gen. Ulysses S. Grant, Acting Secretary of War, resigned.

14 1909: President Theodore Roosevelt wrote to his son: "I have had a great run for my money, and I should have liked to stay in as President if I had felt it was right for me to do so."

15 1929: The Senate ratified the Kellogg-Briand Treaty, by which 49 governments agreed to abolish war as an instrument of national policy.

16 1883: The Pendleton Act became effective. The act established a Civil Service Commission which became the foundation of the modern federal civil service.

17 1893: Former President Rutherford B. Hayes died and was buried in Fremont, Ohio. He was 70 years of age.

18 1903: President Theodore Roosevelt sent the first transatlantic wireless message, to King Edward of England from the Marconi station in Wellfleet, Massachusetts.

19 1931: The National Commission on Law Observance and Enforcement, the Wickersham Commission, reported to President Hoover that national Prohibition was not working.

20 1953: President Dwight D. Eisenhower was inaugurated, the first Republican President to take office since Herbert Hoover was inaugurated in 1929.

21 1950: Alger Hiss was found guilty of disloyalty and of falsifying testimony; Richard Nixon was primarily responsible for obtaining evidence against Hiss.

22 1932: President Hoover signed the bill that created the Reconstruction Finance Corporation, an agency largely responsible for fighting the Great Depression.

23 1948: Gen. Dwight D. Eisenhower, President of Columbia University, told political leaders that he was not a candidate for the presidential nomination.

24 1955: President Eisenhower asked Congress for the authority to use armed force if necessary to assure the security of Formosa and the Pescadores.

25 1864: President Lincoln and Secretary of the Treasury Salmon Chase made final revisions to new regulations for trade.

26 1918: Herbert Hoover was appointed U.S. Food Administrator. He immediately asked for wheatless meals and porkless days as he began plans to stimulate food production.

27 1964: Senator Margaret Chase Smith of Maine announced she would seek the Republican presidential nomination, making her the first woman to seek the presidential nomination of a major political party.

28 1955: The U.S. Senate, by a vote of 85 to 3, voted to support President Eisenhower's request to use armed force if necessary to protect the security of Formosa and the Pescadores.

29 1843: William McKinley, 25th President of the United States, was born in Niles, Ohio, the seventh of nine children.

30 1875: The Hawaiian Reciprocity Treaty, which gave the U.S. the exclusive right to enter Pearl Harbor, was signed by President Ulysses S. Grant.

31 1875: Former President Andrew Johnson died while serving as a senator from Tennessee. He was 66 years old.

FEBRUARY

1 1922: The Five Power Naval Treaty was signed at Washington by representatives of the U.S., Great Britain, Japan, France, and Italy. The treaty froze naval armaments at the status quo in hope of ending the worldwide armaments race.

2 1932: A general disarmament conference assembled at Geneva, Switzerland, with U.S. participation, under the auspices of the League of Nations. When the U.S. proposal for the abolition of all offensive armaments failed, President Hoover proposed a 30 percent overall reduction.

3 1865: President Lincoln and Secretary of State Seward conducted the Hampton Roads Peace Conference for four hours aboard the Union transport ship *River Queen*, discussing ways to end the Civil War.

4 1901: A campaign to eradicate yellow fever was begun in Cuba by Maj. William C. Gorgas of the U.S. Army. Because of his efforts, and those of Dr. Walter Reed, this deadly disease was conquered, subsequently enabling construction of the Panama Canal.

5 1900: The first Hay-Pauncefote Treaty regarding the Panama Canal was signed. Great Britain agreed to renounce all joint rights to a canal which the U.S. was to construct, control, and maintain.

6 1900: Judge William Howard Taft was appointed chairman of the Philippine Commission to establish civil government in the Philippines.

7 1948: Gen. Dwight D. Eisenhower resigned his post as Army Chief of Staff. He was succeeded by Gen. Omar Bradley.

8 1900: A Commercial Reciprocity Treaty was signed by Italy and the U.S.

9 1839: Abraham Lincoln, as a member of the Illinois Legislature, voted for a salary raise for Supreme Court Justices of Illinois, to a level of $1,500 per year.

10 1927: President Calvin Coolidge called for a conference to limit naval armaments. The conference met in Geneva, Switzerland, in June, but France and Italy refused to attend and Great Britain, Japan, and the U.S. were unable to reach an agreement.

11 1861: Lincoln bade farewell to Springfield, Illinois, in a famous speech, observing that "All the strange checkered past seems to crowd now upon my mind . . . let us confidently hope that all will yet be well."

12 1870: The Utah Legislature passed a women's suffrage bill granting full voting rights to women.

13 1861: Lincoln visited Columbus, Ohio, on his way to Washington. He addressed a joint session of the state legislature and at 4:30 p.m. learned by telegram that he was the duly elected President of the United States.

14 1903: President Theodore Roosevelt signed the law creating the Department of Commerce and Labor, the ninth Cabinet office. In 1913 the department was divided into two separate departments.

15 1879: President Rutherford B. Hayes signed into law an act admitting women to practice before the United States Supreme Court.

16 1862: Gen. Ulysses S. Grant earned the nickname "Unconditional Surrender" Grant for responding to Confederate generals with the phrase: "No terms except unconditional surrender."

17 1906: Alice Roosevelt, daughter of the President, married Congressman Nicholas Longworth of Ohio in a White House ceremony. Longworth was later to serve as Speaker of the House of Representatives.

18 1909: President Theodore Roosevelt called a North American Conservation Conference to study natural resources.

19 1861: In New York City, Abraham Lincoln met a Republican delegation that included William Cullen Bryant, editor of the New York *Evening Post*.

20 1912: President William Howard Taft and former President Roosevelt split. Both men planned to seek the Republican presidential nomination in 1912.

21 1898: A naval court of inquiry reported that the battleship U.S.S. *Maine* had been sunk in Havana harbor by the explosion of a submarine mine. This prompted strong public pressure to intervene in Cuba against Spain.

22 1861: Lincoln spoke at a flag-raising ceremony at Independence Hall in Philadelphia, saying: "I'm filled with deep emotion—standing here where were collected the wisdom, patriotism, the devotion to principle from which sprang the institutions under which we live."

23 1904: The Panama Canal Treaty was ratified by the Senate.

24 1868: The Covode Resolution passed the House, impeaching President Andrew Johnson on 11 charges, including violation of the Tenure of Office Act and attempting to bring disgrace and ridicule upon Congress.

25 1870: Hiram R. Revels, Senator from Mississippi, took his seat, becoming the first black to serve in the U.S. Congress. The first black to serve in the House was J.H. Rainey of South Carolina, who also took his seat in 1870.

26 1926: President Calvin Coolidge signed the Revenue Act, which provided for reductions in income taxes, surtaxes, and taxes on passenger cars, and also abolished many nuisance taxes.

27 1922: The 19th Amendment, the Women's Suffrage Amendment, was declared constitutional by a unanimous decision of the Supreme Court.

28 1854: A group of Whigs and Free Soil Democrats met in a Congregational Church in Ripon, Wisconsin, and formed a political organization that would become known as the Republican Party. The word "Republican" was used for the first time to describe their principles.

29 1864: President Lincoln sent an autographed copy of the Gettysburg Address to George Bancroft for the Baltimore Sanitary Fair.

MARCH

1 1875: The Civil Rights Law was enacted, guaranteeing equal rights in public places without distinction of race and forbidding the exclusion of blacks from jury duty.

2 1867: The Office of Education was established as a government department.

3 1865: President Lincoln signed the bill creating the Freedmen's Bureau, which provided relief for former slaves.

4 1917: Jeanette Rankin (R-Mont.) was seated in the House of Representatives, becoming the first woman to serve in either house of Congress.

5 1877: Rutherford B. Hayes was inaugurated as the 19th President of the United States. He was sworn into office on March 3 and inaugurated on March 5, since March 4, the official date of inauguration, fell on a Sunday.

6 1857: The Dred Scott decision was handed down by the Supreme Court, which implied that Congress had no power to exclude slavery from the territories. This quickened the northern moral conscience and contributed to the growth of the Republican Party.

7 1864: President Lincoln issued the order establishing Iowa's western border as the starting point for the Union Pacific Railroad.

8 1841: Oliver Wendell Holmes II, the great justice of the United States Supreme Court, was born.

9 1883: The Civil Service Commission, created by the Pendleton Act, was organized. Dorman Eaton was named chairman.

10 1864: Gen. Ulysses S. Grant was named commander of all Union armies by President Lincoln.

11 1930: William Howard Taft, former President and Chief Justice of the Supreme Court, was buried in Arlington Cemetery. He was the first President to be buried there.

12 1945: Governor Thomas E. Dewey of New York signed a bill establishing a permanent commission to eliminate discrimination in employment, making his state a pioneer in this area.

13 1868: The trial of Andrew Johnson on articles of impeachment began in the Senate, with Chief Justice Salmon Chase presiding. The vote to remove Johnson from office fell one vote short of the needed two-thirds majority.

14 1904: The Supreme Court handed down the famous Northern Securities Company ruling. The case established Theodore Roosevelt's reputation as a "trustbuster."

15 1862: President Lincoln interviewed Senator Solomon Foot (R-Vt.) regarding appropriations for the Capitol dome, which Lincoln wished to continue building as a sign that the Union would go on.

16 1882: The Senate ratified the Geneva Convention on the care of wounded soldiers and the protection of hospitals and medical personnel in time of war.

17 1953: The federal government ended price controls set up during World War II.

18 1924: The House of Representatives passed a Soldiers' Bonus Bill for World War I veterans.

19 1920: The U.S. Senate rejected the Treaty of Versailles, primarily for its provision for U.S. membership in the League of Nations. More Republican senators supported Democratic President Wilson on this issue than did Democratic senators.

20 1854: Major B. Bovey of Wisconsin, after the passage of the Kansas-Nebraska Act, called another meeting at the Ripon Church. All who attended left as "Republicans."

21 1866: Congress authorized the establishment of homes for disabled officers and soldiers.

22 1930: Edward L. Doheny, accused of bribing Secretary of the Interior Albert B. Fall in the Teapot Dome Scandal, was acquitted.

23 1929: President Herbert Hoover announced a major modernization of the White House staff procedures to improve their efficiency.

24 1883: The first long-distance telephone service was inaugurated between New York City and Chicago.

25 1959: President Eisenhower sent a special message to Congress requesting an extension of unemployment compensation benefits.

26 1865: President Lincoln visited General Grant's headquarters and met with Admiral Porter to discuss plans for ending the Civil War.

27 1863: President Lincoln assured visiting Indian chiefs of the government's desire to be fair in its observance of its treaties.

28 1865: General Grant, General Sherman, Admiral Porter, and President Lincoln conferred on the *River Queen* regarding the military situation.

29 1865: Lincoln, continuing his stay at City Point, Virginia, heard two hours of heavy cannonade and musket fire.

30 1867: Secretary of State William H. Seward concluded a treaty with Russia to purchase Alaska for 7.2 million dollars. Called "Seward's Folly," the purchase proved to be Seward's triumph.

31 1870: Thomas P. Mundy became the first black to vote under the provisions of the 15th Amendment when he voted in a municipal election in Perth Amboy, New Jersey.

APRIL

1 1953: The Department of Health, Education, and Welfare was formally created by joint congressional action. On April 11, Mrs. Oveta Culp Hobby was sworn in as the first Secretary of HEW.
2 1866: President Andrew Johnson declared the Civil War ended in Georgia, South Carolina, North Carolina, Virginia, Louisiana, Arkansas, and Florida.
3 1865: Lincoln and Grant conferred at Petersburg, Virginia, and Lincoln expressed his satisfaction with the prospects for an early end to the war.
4 1951: Gen. Dwight D. Eisenhower assumed command of SHAPE (Supreme Headquarters, Allied Powers in Europe), established in Paris.
5 1865: President Lincoln met with former Justice John A. Campbell to discuss how Virginia might be brought back into the Union.
6 1897: Theodore Roosevelt was appointed Assistant Secretary of the Navy by President McKinley.
7 1927: In the first successful demonstration of television, Secretary of Commerce Herbert Hoover saw and heard the president of AT&T, W.S. Gifford, in a broadcast from New York to Washington.
8 1865: General Grant asked Gen. Robert E. Lee to surrender. Lee asked Grant to stipulate the terms of surrender.
9 1865: General Lee surrendered to General Grant at Appomattox Court House, Virginia, effectively ending the Civil War.
10 1872: Governor J. Sterling Morton of Nebraska, concerned about his state's tree shortage, inaugurated Arbor Day as a festival of tree planting.
11 1898: President McKinley sent a message to Congress asking for authority to intervene in Cuban affairs.
12 1861: The bombardment of Fort Sumter in Charleston harbor marked the beginning of the Civil War.
13 1865: General Sherman's Army of the Tennessee occupied Raleigh, North Carolina.
14 1865: President Lincoln, attending a performance of *Our American Cousin* at Ford's Theatre, was shot by assassin John Wilkes Booth.
15 1865: Vice President Andrew Johnson was sworn in as the 17th President of the United States only three hours after Lincoln's death.
16 1862: President Lincoln signed a bill freeing slaves in the District of Columbia.
17 1917: Senator William M. Calder of New York introduced a bill before the Senate which would have authorized daylight saving time. The bill was defeated.

18 1864: President Lincoln commuted the court-martial sentences of 20 men condemned to be shot.
19 1861: President Lincoln ordered the blockade of southern ports.
20 1898: A joint resolution of Congress recognized the independence of Cuba and demanded that Spain relinquish its authority and withdraw its land and sea forces.
21 1862: General Grant was given command of the Army of the Tennessee.
22 1864: Congress authorized the director of the U.S. Mint to use the motto "In God We Trust" on all coins.
23 1898: The U.S. government issued a call for 125,000 volunteer troops to fight the war with Spain.
24 1877: Northern rule in the South and the period of Reconstruction came to an end as President Hayes ordered the removal of federal troops from New Orleans.
25 1898: Congress declared war on Spain.
26 1910: Dedication ceremonies were held at the Pan-American Union in Washington, D.C., where President Taft and Andrew Carnegie planted the Tree of Peace and dedicated it to friendship among the American republics.
27 1822: Ulysses S. Grant, General of the Army and later 18th President, was born in Point Pleasant, Ohio.
28 1904: Congress passed an act for the temporary government of the Panama Canal Zone.
29 1931: President Hoover received King Prjadhipok of Siam, the first monarch to visit the United States.
30 1900: Congress passed an act to provide for the territorial government of the Hawaiian Islands.

MAY

1 1901: The Pan-American Exposition opened in Buffalo, New York.
2 1865: President Andrew Johnson offered a reward of 100,000 dollars for the capture of Jefferson Davis, former President of the Confederacy.
3 1865: President Lincoln's body arrived in Springfield, Illinois, completing a 1,700-mile journey home from Washington, D.C. A century later, Carl Sandburg said, "The American people wept as never before."
4 1865: President Lincoln was buried in Springfield; Bishop Matthew Simpson delivered the final funeral sermon.
5 1959: President Eisenhower sent a message of sympathy to President Echegoyen on the Uruguayian flood disaster and made commitments to help alleviate the crisis.
6 1898: Theodore Roosevelt organized the famous Rough Riders, which he later led up Cuba's San Juan Hill during the Spanish-American War.

7 1889: Theodore Roosevelt was appointed to the Civil Service Commission by President Benjamin Harrison. He served six years on the commission.

8 1871: The Treaty of Washington was signed between the United States and Great Britain providing for international arbitration of claims arising from the Civil War.

9 1854: Gen. Israel Washburne called a meeting of 30 congressmen to form a political party against slavery; the name Republican was selected.

10 1869: Former California Governor Leland Stanford drove home the golden spike at Promontory, Utah, celebrating the completion of the first transcontinental railroad.

11 1910: Glacier National Park, in Montana, was created by an act of Congress.

12 1863: Lincoln received confirmation of the death of Confederate Gen. Stonewall Jackson.

13 1954: President Eisenhower signed the bill authorizing the construction of the St. Lawrence Seaway.

14 1908: The White House Conservation Conference called by President Theodore Roosevelt was attended by 44 governors.

15 1862: Congress created the Department of Agriculture, which was given Cabinet rank in 1889.

16 1860: The Republican National Convention that nominated Lincoln convened in Chicago.

17 1877: Former President Ulysses S. Grant began his historic tour of the world.

18 1860: Abraham Lincoln of Illinois and Hannibal Hamlin of Maine were nominated as the candidates of the Republican Party for President and Vice President.

19 1856: Senator Charles Sumner of Massachusetts delivered his famous "Crime Against Kansas" speech in the Senate. Three days later he was assaulted at his Senate desk by Congressman Preston Brooks of South Carolina and beaten unconscious with a cane.

20 1862: President Lincoln signed the Homestead Act, which provided landless settlers with 160 free acres if they lived on and cultivated the land for five years.

21 1874: Nellie Grant, daughter of President and Mrs. Grant, was married in the White House to Englishman Algernon Sartoris.

22 1870: An act to create the Department of Justice was passed by Congress. The Attorney General was named head of the department, although that office had been created by Congress in 1789 and had become a Cabinet position in 1814.

23 1860: Abraham Lincoln formally accepted the Republican nomination for President.

24 1959: President Eisenhower issued a statement of tribute, respect, and gratitude for the services of John Foster Dulles on the latter's death.

25 1960: President Eisenhower made a radio and television report to the American people from Paris, France.

26 1868: The Senate move to impeach President Andrew Johnson failed by one vote to achieve the necessary two-thirds majority.

27 1961: John Tower, with his election to the seat formerly held by Lyndon Johnson, became the first Republican Senator from Texas since Reconstruction.

28 1908: Congress passed a child labor law for the District of Columbia.

29 1865: President Andrew Johnson issued a proclamation of amnesty granting pardons to Southerners.

30 1908: Congress passed a Workmen's Compensation Act for railroad and government employees.

31 1870: The First Enforcement Act was passed by a Republican Congress to prevent the 15th Amendment from being abridged by violence from secret societies.

JUNE

1 1902: The permanent Census Office was established.

2 1924: By an act of Congress, all Indians born in the United States were granted full U.S. citizenship.

3 1863: Congress passed a law establishing the national banking system to help finance the Civil War.

4 1924: An eternal light was illuminated in New York City's Madison Square in memory of New York soldiers who died in World War I.

5 1872: Ulysses S. Grant and Henry Wilson were nominated for President and Vice President by the Republican Party in Philadelphia, Pennsylvania.

6 1908: President Theodore Roosevelt appointed a conservation committee of 57 members, with Gifford Pinchot named as chairman.

7 1864: The Republican nominating convention convened in Baltimore, Maryland. The next day, President Lincoln was renominated for a second term, with Andrew Johnson of Tennessee nominated for Vice President.

8 1908: President Theodore Roosevelt's efforts to mediate the Russo-Japanese War, which culminated in the Treaty of Portsmouth, earned him the Nobel Peace Prize.

9 1959: President Eisenhower made a speech at the National Conference on Civil Rights.

10 1920: The Water Power Act established a Federal Power Commission consisting of the Secretaries of War, Interior, and Agriculture.

11 1927: Charles A. Lindbergh was welcomed home after his historic flight across the Atlantic; President Coolidge presented Lindbergh with the first Distinguished Flying Cross.

12 1945: Gen. Dwight D. Eisenhower was given a grand reception in England and awarded the Freedom of London award.

13 1866: The 14th Amendment, proclaiming that citizens' rights were not to be abridged, was formally proposed and referred to the states for ratification. It was declared part of the Constitution on July 28, 1866.

14 1922: President Warren G. Harding became the first President to speak over the radio, at the dedication of the Francis Scott Key memorial at Fort McHenry in Baltimore, Maryland.

15 1929: The Agriculture Marketing Act was passed, authorizing establishment of the Farm Board to promote farm product sales.

16 1876: Rutherford B. Hayes of Ohio and William A. Wheeler of New York were nominated by the Republican National Convention for President and Vice President.

17 1902: The Reclamation Act was passed by Congress, giving the President the authority to retain public lands as part of the public domain, thereby initiating the federal park system.

18 1945: Gen. Dwight D. Eisenhower was given a hero's welcome in Washington, D.C., following his return from Europe.

19 1862: Congress passed an act prohibiting slavery in various territories of the United States.

20 1931: President Herbert Hoover proposed a one-year international debt moratorium to help ease the increasingly ominous world financial situation.

21 1955: The reciprocal Trade Agreements Act was extended to June 30, 1958, by the House of Representatives.

22 1902: President Theodore Roosevelt issued a proclamation setting aside Mount Graham as a forest reserve in Arizona and designating Lincoln Reserve in New Mexico.

23 1958: President Eisenhower sent a special message to Congress transmitting the international agreement between the United States and Euratom.

24 1954: Colorado Springs, Colorado, was named the site for the new Air Force Academy.

25 1868: Congressional representation was granted to six former states of the Confederacy: North Carolina, South Carolina, Louisiana, Georgia, Alabama, and Florida.

26 1884: A congressional act was passed to grant the commission of ensign to all Naval Academy graduates.

27 1884: The new U.S. Bureau of Labor became part of the Department of the Interior.

28 1902: The Isthmian Canal Act was passed by Congress, authorizing the financing and construction of a canal across the Isthmus of Panama.

29 1906: The Railroad Rate Bill, giving the federal government the authority to set rates for interstate shipments, was passed by Congress.

30 1906: President Theodore Roosevelt signed the Pure Food and Drug Act.

JULY

1 1898: Col. Theodore Roosevelt's volunteer regiment, the Rough Riders, led the charge up San Juan Hill in Cuba during the Spanish-American War.

2 1862: President Lincoln signed the Morrill Act distributing public land to the states to establish land-grant colleges.

3 1898: The U.S. Navy defeated the Spanish fleet outside the harbor of Santiago, Cuba.

4 1872: Calvin Coolidge, 30th President, was born in Plymouth, Vermont.

5 1932: A bill was passed authorizing the distribution of government wheat and cotton to the National American Red Cross.

6 1854: The first Republican convention was held under the oaks in Jackson, Michigan.

7 1958: President Eisenhower signed the bill for Alaskan statehood. He issued a formal proclamation of Alaska's official recognition as a state in 1959.

8 1863: With the capture of Fort Hudson, Union forces controlled the Mississippi River.

9 1856: John C. Frémont formally accepted the nomination as the Republican Party's first presidential candidate.

10 1833: Abraham Lincoln was mustered out of the Illinois militia after serving in the Black Hawk campaign.

11 1905: Russia and Japan accepted President Theodore Roosevelt's proposal for peace talks at Portsmouth, New Hampshire.

12 1954: A four-point program of interstate highway modernization was proposed by President Eisenhower. The cost, several billions of dollars, would be shared by federal and state governments.

13 1854: The Republican state convention in Madison, Wisconsin, nominated a full ticket for the fall elections. Republicans subsequently carried the state.

14 1890: Congress passed the Sherman Silver Purchase Act, requiring the government to purchase 4.5 million ounces of silver per month and to issue paper notes against it.

15 1964: Margaret Chase Smith (R-Me.) became the first woman presidential candidate of a major political party to have her name put in nomination.

16 1954: President Eisenhower signed a bill increasing the reenlistment bonus for members of the uniformed services.

17 1862: President Lincoln was empowered to draft soldiers for the first time in U.S. history.

18 1932: A treaty was signed between the United States and Canada calling for the joint operation of

the St. Lawrence River. It was not until the 1950s that actual construction of the St. Lawrence Seaway began.

19 1959: President Eisenhower sent a message to Congress with the tenth annual report on the United Nations.

20 1902: President Theodore Roosevelt received and sent to Congress the commission report recommending the purchase of property and rights to the Panama Canal for 40 million dollars.

21 1930: The U.S. Veterans Administration was established.

22 1932: The Federal Home Loan Bank Act, recommended by President Herbert Hoover, was passed and implemented.

23 1885: Ulysses S. Grant, former President of the United States, died at age 63 and was buried in New York City.

24 1929: President Herbert Hoover proclaimed the Kellogg-Briand Treaty in force, by which 49 nations agreed to renounce war as an instrument of national policy.

25 1866: Ulysses S. Grant was named General of the Army, the first American officer raised to that rank.

26 1882: The Geneva Convention of 1864, outlining the treatment of war casualties, was accepted by the United States. Clara Barton, founder of the American branch of the Red Cross, did much to promote public sentiment in favor of ratifying the Geneva Convention.

27 1953: The Korean War ended with the signing of the armistice at Panmunjom by representatives of the United Nations and the Communist powers.

28 1868: The 14th Amendment was ratified, granting U.S. citizenship to all persons born in or naturalized in the U.S. regardless of race, creed, or national origin.

29 1899: The U.S. signed and announced adherence to the Hague Convention, which created a permanent court of arbitration later superseded by the World Court.

30 1956: "In God We Trust" officially became the U.S. motto.

31 1953: Senator Robert A. Taft of Ohio, son of William Howard Taft and majority leader of the Senate, died in New York City.

AUGUST

1 1953: President Eisenhower proposed widening the Social Security Act to cover another ten and a half million persons. Legislation was subsequently passed in 1954.

2 1927: President Calvin Coolidge made his famous "I do not choose to run" statement to the press summoned to the Black Hills, in South Dakota.

3 1923: Vice President Calvin Coolidge was sworn in as President by his father in Plymouth, Vermont, where the news of President Harding's death had reached them.

4 1834: Abraham Lincoln, in his second try for public office, was elected to the Illinois House of Representatives.

5 1867: President Andrew Johnson asked for the resignation of Secretary of War Edwin Stanton, whom he suspected of blocking Reconstruction.

6 1959: President Eisenhower signed the bill to amend the Tennessee Valley Authority Act.

7 1927: The International Peace Bridge at Buffalo, New York, was dedicated, commemorating more than a hundred years of peace between the United States and Canada.

8 1953: The United States signed a mutual security pact with the Republic of Korea.

9 1905: The peace conference called by President Theodore Roosevelt to mediate the differences between Japan and Russia convened in Portsmouth, New Hampshire.

10 1874: Herbert Hoover, 31st President of the United States, was born in West Branch, Iowa.

11 1902: Oliver Wendell Holmes was appointed to the Supreme Court by President Theodore Roosevelt.

12 1898: A Peace Protocol was signed by the United States and Spain, bringing the Spanish-American War to an end.

13 1912: Congress approved an act authorizing the President to take over all U.S. radio communication in time of war.

14 1959: President Eisenhower signed the Labor, Health, Education, and Welfare appropriation bill.

15 1921: The Packers and Stockyards Act, forbidding unfair and discriminatory practices, was passed.

16 1902: President Theodore Roosevelt issued a proclamation setting aside Little Belt Mountain and Madison Forest Reserve, in Montana.

17 1907: Secretary of War William Howard Taft concluded agreements with Colombia and Panama regarding the Panama Canal.

18 1954: Assistant Secretary of Labor James E. Wilkins became the first black to ever attend a Cabinet meeting.

19 1862: President Lincoln received Horace Greeley's letter regarding emancipation.

20 1833: Benjamin Harrison, 23rd President of the United States, was born near North Bend, Ohio.

21 1858: The first Lincoln-Douglas debate was held at Ottawa, Illinois.

22 1956: President Dwight D. Eisenhower and Vice President Richard M. Nixon were renominated for second terms at the Republican National Convention in San Francisco.

23 1912: The Bureau of Foreign and Domestic Commerce was created.

24 1912: President William Howard Taft approved the

act organizing the territory of Alaska and granting it self-government.

25 1921: The U.S. signed the treaty of peace in Berlin, officially ending the state of war with Germany.

26 1920: A formal proclamation was issued by Secretary of State Bainbridge Colby noting the ratification of the 19th Amendment, which granted women the right to vote.

27 1928: Fifteen nations signed the Kellogg-Briand Peace Pact in Paris.

28 1958: The Agriculture Act modified price supports on basic crops for 1959 and 1960, giving farmers the choice between price supports and increased crop allotments.

29 1958: President Eisenhower signed the Euratom Cooperation Act, intended to develop nuclear power through international cooperation with Europe.

30 1924: The Dawes Plan for World War I reparations was signed in London, in accordance with suggestions by U.S. Ambassador Charles G. Dawes.

31 1910: Theodore Roosevelt delivered his famous New Nationalism speech at Osawatomie, Kansas, in which he proclaimed the Square Deal as his policy.

SEPTEMBER

1 1958: President Eisenhower addressed American labor, listing the principles and guarantees needed for good labor relations.

2 1901: The phrase "big stick" became Theodore Roosevelt's trademark following his remark at the Minnesota State Fair: "Speak softly and carry a big stick; you will go far."

3 1954: President Eisenhower signed the Espionage and Sabotage Act, authorizing the death penalty for peacetime sabotage.

4 1957: President Eisenhower signed a joint resolution to commemorate the 100th anniversary of Theodore Roosevelt's birth.

5 1905: President Theodore Roosevelt's peace talks succeeded with the Treaty of Portsmouth, ending the Russo-Japanese War. Roosevelt later won the Nobel Peace Prize for his efforts at mediation.

6 1901: President William McKinley was shot by a demented anarchist while attending the Pan-American Exposition in Buffalo, New York. He died on September 14.

7 1861: President Lincoln received Baron de Stoeckl, Russian minister who offered a strong statement of friendship.

8 1858: Abraham Lincoln delivered a speech in Clinton, Illinois, in which he uttered the immortal phrase: "You can fool all of the people some of the time; some of the people all the time; but not all of the people all of the time."

9 1957: The first Civil Rights Act since 1875 was passed, establishing a bipartisan commission to investigate abuses of equal protection under the law and violations of voting rights.

10 1959: President Eisenhower delivered a radio and television report to the American people on his European trip.

11 1861: President Lincoln ordered General Frémont to modify his emancipation proclamation of August 30 to conform with the act of Congress.

12 1906: President Theodore Roosevelt ordered a warship to Cuba; marines landed the following day.

13 1948: Margaret Chase Smith was elected to the Senate by Maine voters.

14 1901: Theodore Roosevelt was sworn in as the 26th President shortly after President William McKinley's death on this day.

15 1857: William Howard Taft was born, the only American to serve both as President (the 27th) and as Chief Justice of the Supreme Court.

16 1959: President Eisenhower addressed a group of foreign educators participating in the International Teacher Development Program.

17 1898: The Peace Commission appointed by President McKinley sailed for Paris to negotiate the treaty ending the Spanish-American War.

18 1862: President Lincoln appointed Jacob Frankel as an Army chaplain, the first American Rabbi to hold such office.

19 1901: President McKinley was buried in Canton, Ohio.

20 1881: Chester A. Arthur became the 21st President following President Garfield's death from gunshot wounds he suffered on July 1, 1881.

21 1881: President Garfield's body was lain in state in the Capitol Rotunda.

22 1922: The Cable Act declared that women no longer would be deprived of citizenship upon marriage to an alien.

23 1862: The preliminary draft of the Emancipation Proclamation was issued by President Lincoln.

24 1957: President Eisenhower sent some one thousand Army paratroopers to Little Rock, Arkansas, to enforce school desegregation.

25 1890: Congress established Yosemite National Park in California.

26 1960: Presidential candidates Richard Nixon and John F. Kennedy discussed the election issues in a televised debate.

27 1959: President Eisenhower issued a joint statement with Russian Premier Khrushchev at the end of the Camp David conference.

28 1909: President William Howard Taft set aside three million acres of western land for conservation purposes.

29 1906: The Platt Amendment was invoked in Cuba; the U.S. assumed military control, with Secretary

of War Taft being named Provisional Governor.

30 1867: The Midway Islands were acquired as vital links in U.S. Pacific defenses.

OCTOBER

1 1890: Congress created the Weather Bureau within the Department of Agriculture. Previously weather information had come from the Army Signal Corps.

2 1889: Secretary of State James G. Blaine presided over the First International Conference of American States, which met in Washington, D.C. The conference laid the foundation for what later became the Pan-American Union.

3 1863: President Lincoln proclaimed the first national day of Thanksgiving, to be observed on the last Thursday in November.

4 1822: Rutherford B. Hayes, 19th President of the United States, was born near Delaware, Ohio.

5 1830: Chester A. Arthur, 21st President of the United States, was born at Union, Vermont.

6 1884: The Naval War College was established by the Navy Department at Newport, Rhode Island. Its first superintendent was Comdr. Stephen Bleecker Luce.

7 1858: The fifth Lincoln-Douglas debate was held at Galesburg, Illinois.

8 1903: A commercial treaty with China was signed by the U.S.

9 1959: President Eisenhower reassured Prime Minister Erbal of Iran that the U.S. would continue to support the collective efforts of Iran and other nations to maintain their independence.

10 1929: The U.S. State Department accepted an invitation to the London Naval Conference to discuss naval disarmament.

11 1960: President Eisenhower greeted the King and Queen of Denmark and paid tribute to immigrants from Denmark.

12 1871: A proclamation against the Ku Klux Klan was issued by President Grant.

13 1858: The sixth Lincoln-Douglas debate was held in Quincy, Illinois.

14 1890: Dwight D. Eisenhower, 34th President of the United States, was born in Denison, Texas.

15 1858: The seventh and final Lincoln-Douglas debate was held at Alton, Illinois.

16 1854: Lincoln and Douglas met in Peoria, Illinois, where Lincoln made one of his first great speeches.

17 1953: President Eisenhower spoke in New Orleans at the commemoration of the 150th anniversary of the Louisiana Purchase.

18 1901: President Theodore Roosevelt entertained Booker T. Washington with dinner. The noted black educator was the first black to be a guest in the White House.

19 1960: President Eisenhower announced an agreement with Canada regarding water resources in the Columbia River basin.

20 1960: The U.S. State Department placed an embargo on exports to Cuba; some medicines and foods were excluded from the embargo.

21 1960: Vice President Richard M. Nixon and Senator John F. Kennedy met in their last televised debate.

22 1901: The Second Pan-American Congress was opened in Mexico City.

23 1955: President Eisenhower wrote Vice President Nixon and the Cabinet concerning the task of Secretary of State Dulles at that summer's Geneva conference.

24 1932: The Regional Agricultural Credit Corporation was chartered at Albany, New York.

25 1954: For the first time, a Cabinet meeting was televised. President Eisenhower and the Cabinet heard a report from Secretary of State Dulles on the recent Paris conference.

26 1901: An extradition treaty was signed by Belgium and the U.S.

27 1858: Theodore Roosevelt, 26th President of the United States, was born in New York City.

28 1954: President Eisenhower and Chancellor Adenauer of Germany issued a joint statement on the problems of Germany and Europe.

29 1953: President Eisenhower addressed the American Forest Congress on the importance of the conservation of natural resources.

30 1912: James S. Sherman died during the presidential campaign; he was succeeded as the Republican candidate for Vice President by Nicholas Murray Butler.

31 1932: Herbert Hoover campaigned for reelection by speaking at Madison Square Garden in New York City.

NOVEMBER

1 1884: By international agreement, the Greenwich Meridian was designated the prime meridian for determining time zones.

2 1865: Warren G. Harding, 29th President of the United States, was born at Corsica, Ohio.

3 1908: William Howard Taft and James S. Sherman, Republicans, were elected President and Vice President.

4 1924: Calvin Coolidge and Charles G. Dawes, Republicans, were elected President and Vice President.

5 1872: President Ulysses S. Grant was reelected President and Henry Wilson was elected Vice President.

6 1860: Abraham Lincoln and Hannibal Hamlin, Republicans, were elected President and Vice President.

7 1854: Abraham Lincoln was elected to the Illinois Legislature but resigned on November 27th to become a candidate for the U.S. Senate.

8 1898: Theodore Roosevelt was nominated and elected to the governorship of New York on the Republican ticket. He was chosen for his outstanding record and his strength of character.

9 1906: Theodore Roosevelt became the first U.S. President to leave the country while in office when he sailed on the battleship U.S.S. *Louisiana* to visit the Isthmus of Panama and inspect the canal.

10 1954: The Marine Memorial, depicting the flag-raising on Iwo Jima during World War II, was dedicated at Arlington National Cemetery in Arlington, Virginia.

11 1921: President Warren G. Harding dedicated the Tomb of the Unknown Soldier in Arlington National Cemetery.

12 1921: President Warren G. Harding and Secretary of State Charles Evans Hughes convened the Washington Disarmament Conference.

13 1956: The Supreme Court ruled that racial segregation on public buses was unconstitutional.

14 1935: The Philippine Islands were declared a free commonwealth, fulfilling the promise made by the U.S. on their acquisition as a result of the Spanish-American War.

15 1906: President Theodore Roosevelt applied the terms of the Sherman Antitrust Act to Standard Oil of New Jersey and 70 other corporations.

16 1864: General Sherman left Atlanta to resume his march to the sea.

17 1949: Alger Hiss was found guilty of perjury and sentenced to five years in prison largely as a result of an investigation by Congressman Richard M. Nixon.

18 1901: The second Hay-Pauncefote Treaty was signed, by which the British consented to American control of the Isthmian Canal. On the same day in 1903, the Hay-Banau-Varilla Treaty was signed, giving the U.S. full control over a ten-mile-wide strip in which to build the canal.

19 1863: President Abraham Lincoln delivered the Gettysburg Address at the dedication of the Gettysburg battlefield as a national cemetery.

20 1960: President Eisenhower issued a statement on the report of the Science Advisory Committees.

21 1864: President Lincoln wrote Mrs. Lydia Bixby of Boston to offer his sympathy for her loss of five sons in the war.

22 1927: An extradition treaty was signed by Poland and the U.S.

23 1921: The Sheppard-Towner Act was signed by President Harding, extending federal aid to the states for maternity and infancy care.

24 1863: A national day of Thanksgiving, suggested by President Washington in 1789, was proclaimed by President Lincoln. Since then Congress has approved the fourth Thursday in November as the official Thanksgiving Day.

25 1955: Racial segregation on interstate trains and buses was banned by the Interstate Commerce Commission.

26 1861: President Lincoln drafted a bill for compensated emancipation in Delaware, but the bill was never introduced.

27 1930: Frank B. Kellogg, former Secretary of State and a justice on the Permanent Court for International Justice at The Hague, was awarded the Nobel Peace Prize.

28 1955: President Eisenhower called a conference on education, focusing attention on educational needs and goals, teacher training, and school financing.

29 1952: President Eisenhower, carrying out his campaign promise, flew to Korea to investigate the situation there.

30 1908: Secretary of State Elihu Root and Ambassador Takahira of Japan signed the Root-Takahira Agreement of friendship and trade.

DECEMBER

1 1862: President Lincoln sent his second annual message to Congress.

2 1865: Alabama became the 27th state to ratify the 13th Amendment to the Constitution, thereby providing the necessary two-thirds majority to ratify the amendment abolishing slavery.

3 1861: President Lincoln sent his first annual message to Congress.

4 1959: President Eisenhower arrived in Rome on his famous worldwide trip to present American views to the world.

5 1908: An arbitration treaty was signed by Peru and the U.S.

6 1904: President Theodore Roosevelt announced to Congress the doctrine of International Police Power as a corollary to the Monroe Doctrine.

7 1847: In Congress, Abraham Lincoln listened to President James K. Polk's message on the Mexican invasion of Texas; later he questioned Polk on the exact location of the supposed invasion.

8 1863: President Lincoln's Proclamation of Amnesty and Reconstruction offered full pardons to all Southerners who voluntarily took a prescribed loyalty oath.

9 1953: President Eisenhower, in a speech before the General Assembly of the United Nations, proposed the peaceful use of atomic energy.

10 1898: Cuba, Puerto Rico, Guam, and the Philippines were ceded to the United States by the treaty signed in Paris ending the Spanish-American War.

11 1902: A commercial reciprocity treaty was signed by Cuba and the U.S.

12 1906: President Theodore Roosevelt appointed Oscar S. Straus Secretary of Commerce and Labor, the first Jew appointed to a Cabinet position.

13 1922: The Four Power Pacific Treaty was signed at the Washington Disarmament Conference by the United States, Great Britain, France, and Japan.

14 1920: Senator William Borah (R-Idaho) introduced a resolution requesting the President to call an international conference on reduction of naval armaments.

15 1861: President Lincoln studied Cyrus Field's proposal for an underwater telegraph cable to link Washington with coastal forts as far south as Key West, Florida.

16 1901: The Senate ratified the second Hay-Pauncefote Treaty, which provided that the Panama Canal was to be free and open to ships of all nations on equal terms.

17 1862: A delegation of seven Republicans demanded that Lincoln reorganize the Cabinet. The President refused the resignations of Seward and Chase, thereby weathering the crisis.

18 1865: The 13th Amendment formally became part of the Constitution.

19 1929: President Herbert Hoover appointed the Social Research Council.

20 1900: The Senate ratified the first Hay-Pauncefote Treaty; the British, however, refused to accept the treaty due to an amendment allowing the U.S. to fortify the canal.

21 1928: An act authorizing the construction of Boulder Dam was approved by President Coolidge.

22 1864: President Lincoln received a message from General Sherman in Georgia: "I beg to present you as a Christmas gift the city of Savannah."

23 1929: An act authorizing the construction of the Pan-American Union Building in Washington, D.C., was approved by President Hoover.

24 1943: General Eisenhower was appointed commander of Allied forces for the projected invasion of Europe.

25 1921: President Warren G. Harding pardoned Eugene V. Debs, a socialist leader imprisoned for violating a strike law.

26 1863: President Lincoln gave the original draft of the Emancipation Proclamation to the women in charge of the Northwest Sanitary Fair in Chicago.

27 1861: President Lincoln told Charles Sumner that he was preparing an emancipation doctrine.

28 1927: Representatives of 15 nations agreed to the terms of the Kellogg-Briand Pact.

29 1808: Andrew Johnson, 17th President, was born in Raleigh, North Carolina.

30 1890: The Sherman Antitrust Act became law.

31 1903: Republicans announced a record-breaking year of immigration, with 857,046 people entering the country.

In the preceding pages of this book, more than a hundred Republican leaders of the past and present have been discussed. It has been impossible, of course, to cite every important Republican leader, or even to adequately detail the accomplishments of those who have been mentioned. The following list provides the names and brief identifications of a few Republican leaders who merit further attention. We invite you to examine the list, and perhaps add your own selection of names to the ever growing roll call of Republican notables. In subsequent editions, the Republican Heritage Foundation will publish expanded and updated versions of this list incorporating the recommendations of our readers.

Adkins, Bertha (1906-) Educator and administrator. Assistant Chairman of the Republican National Committee, 1953-58. Undersecretary of Health, Education and Welfare, 1958-60.

Alcorn, Meade (1907-) Lawyer and politician. Chairman of the Republican National Committee, 1957.

Arends, Leslie (1895-) Representative from Illinois, 1935-74.

Baker, Howard H., Jr. (1925-) Senator from Tennessee, 1967-85. Senate Majority Leader, 1981-85. White House Chief of Staff, 1987-. Son-in-law of Everett McKinley Dirksen.

Ballinger, Richard A. (1851-1922) Lawyer and Secretary of the Interior under Taft, 1909-11.

Banks, Nathaniel P. (1816-94) Representative from Massachusetts, 1853-57, 1865-73, 1875-79, 1889-91. Speaker of the House, 1853-55. Served as a major general in the Union Army during the Civil War.

Beveridge, Albert J. (1862-1927) Senator from Indiana, 1899-1911. Widely read author and historian.

Bingham, Kinsley S. (1808-61) Representative from Michigan, 1847-51. Elected governor of Michigan, 1854-58, on the first Republican ticket ever. Senator from Michigan, 1859-61.

Bliss, Ray C. (1907-) Chairman of the Republican National Committee, 1965.

Bolton, Frances Payne (1917-1972) Representative from Ohio, 1953-57, 1963-65. Member of House Foreign Affairs Committee.

Brookhart, Smith (1869-1944) Senator from Iowa, 1922-26, 1927-33.

Bush, George (1924-) Representative from Texas, 1967-71. Chairman of the Republican National Committee, 1973-74. Vice President of the United States, 1981-.

Chandler, Zachariah (1813-79) Senator from Michigan, 1857-75. Secretary of the Interior, 1875-77. Chairman of the Republican National Committee, 1876-79.

Cheney, Richard B. (1941-) Representative from Wyoming, 1979-.

Church, Marguerite Stitt (1892-) Representative from Illinois, 1951-63. Member of House Foreign Af-

# of Note

fairs Committee.

Conkling, Roscoe (1829-88) Representative from New York, 1859-63, 1865-67. Senator, 1867-81. Famed for what James G. Blaine called his "turkey gobbler strut."

Cummins, Albert Baird (1850-1926) Governor of Iowa, 1902-1908. Senator from Iowa, 1908-26. President pro tempore, 1919-25.

Curtis, Carl (1905-) Representative from Nebraska, 1939-54. Senator, 1955-79.

Curtis, Charles (1860-1936) Representative from Kansas, 1893-1907. Senator, 1907-13, 1915-29. President pro tempore, 1911. Vice President under Hoover, 1929-33.

Dawes, Charles G. (1865-1951) Lawyer, financier, and politician. Served as a brigadier general in World War I. President of the commission on war reparations. Vice President under Coolidge, 1925-29. Winner of the Nobel Peace Prize, 1925.

Depew, Chauncey M. (1834-1928) President of the New York Central Railroad, 1885-99. Senator from New York, 1899-1911. Renowned after-dinner speaker and wit.

Dickinson, Lester Jesse (1873-1968) Representative from Iowa, 1919-31. Senator, 1931-37.

Dirksen, Everett McKinley (1896-1969) Representative from Illinois, 1933-49. Senator, 1951-69. Legendary for his wit and loquacious eloquence. Affectionately termed the "Wizard of Ooze."

Dole, Robert J. (1923-) Representative from Kansas, 1961-69. Senator, 1969-. Chairman of the Republican National Committee, 1971-73. Senate Majority Leader, 1985-87.

Dolliver, Jonathan P. (1858-1910) Representative from Iowa, 1889-1900. Senator, 1900-10.

Dwyer, Florence Price (1902-1976) Representative from New Jersey, 1959-73. Member of House Banking and Currency Committee.

Evarts, William M. (1818-1901) Attorney General under Andrew Johnson, 1868-69. Secretary of State under Hayes, 1877-81. Senator from New York, 1885-91.

Everett, Edward (1794-1865) Representative from Massachusetts, 1825-35. Governor of Massachusetts, 1836-40. Secretary of State, 1852-53. Senator from Massachusetts, 1853-54. One of the founders of the Republican Party.

Fairbanks, Charles W. (1852-1918) Senator from Indiana, 1897-1905. Vice President under Theodore Roosevelt, 1905-09. Unsuccessful candidate for Vice President, 1916.

Fenwick, Millicent (1910-) Representative from New Jersey, 1975-83.

Fish, Hamilton (1808-93) Representative from New York, 1843-45. Governor of New York, 1849-51. Senator from New York, 1851-57. Secretary of State under Grant, 1869-77.

Ford, Elizabeth (Betty) (1918-) First Lady of the United States, 1974-77.

Frenzel, William E. (1928-) Representative from Minnesota, 1971-.

Grassley, Charles (1933-) Representative from Iowa, 1975-81. Senator, 1981-.

Griffin, Robert P. (1923-) Representative from Michigan, 1957-66. Senator, 1966-79.

Hamlin, Hannibal (1809-91) Representative from Maine, 1843-47. Senator, 1848-57, 1857-61, 1869-81. Lincoln's first Vice President, 1861-65.

Harden, Mrs. Cecil (1894-) Representative from Indiana, 1949-59.

Hatfield, Mark O. (1922-) Governor of Oregon, 1959-67. Senator from Oregon, 1967-.

Hawkins, Paula (1927-) Senator from Florida, 1981-86. Member of Senate Agriculture Committee.

Heckler, Margaret (1931-) Representative from Massachusetts, 1967-83. Secretary of Health and Human Services, 1983-85. Ambassador to Ireland, 1985-.

Heinz, Henry John III (1938-) Representative from Pennsylvania, 1971-77. Senator, 1977-.

Hobby, Oveta Culp (1905-) Parliamentarian of the Texas House of Representatives, 1926-31, 1939, 1941. Secretary of Health, Education and Welfare, 1953-55.

Ingersoll, Robert G. (1833-99) Lawyer. Served in the Union Army during the Civil War. Attorney General of Illinois, 1866-69. Spellbinding orator; gave the famous "Plumed Knight" speech nominating Blaine in 1876.

Judd, Walter (1898-) Representative from Minnesota, 1943-63. Served in the Army during World War I. Medical missionary to China, 1925-31, 1934-38.

Kassebaum, Nancy Landon (1932-) Senator from Kansas, 1978-. Daughter of former Kansas governor and Republican presidential candidate Alf Landon.

Kellogg, Frank B. (1856-1937) Senator from Minnesota, 1917-23. Secretary of State under Coolidge, 1925-29. Coauthor of the Kellogg-Briand Peace Pact, 1928. Awarded Nobel Peace Prize, 1930.

Leach, Jim (1942-) Representative from Iowa, 1977-.

Lenroot, Irvine L. (1869-1949) Representative from Wisconsin, 1909-18. Senator, 1918-27. Judge of the U.S. Court of Customs and Patent Appeals, 1929-44.

Logan, John A. (1826-86) Representative from Illinois, 1859-62, 1867-71. Senator, 1871-77, 1879-86. Served as a major general in the Union Army during the Civil War. Republican nominee for Vice President, 1884.

Lott, Trent (1941-) Representative from Mississippi, 1972-.

Luce, Clare Boothe (1903-87) Journalist and publisher. Representative from Connecticut, 1943-47.

McCormick, Ruth Hanna (1880-1944) Representative from Illinois, 1929-31.

Martin, Joseph W., Jr. (1884-1968) Representative from Massachusetts, 1925-67. Speaker of the House, 1947-49, 1953-55. Chairman of the Republican National Committee, 1940-42.

Martin, Lynn (1939-) Representative from Illinois, 1981-. Member of House Budget Committee.

Mellon, Andrew W. (1855-1937) Banker, financier, and philanthropist. Secretary of the Treasury under Harding, Coolidge, and Hoover, 1921-31. Ambassador to Great Britain, 1931-32. Established the National Gallery of Art, 1937.

Michel, Robert H. (1923-) Representative from Illinois, 1957-. House Minority Leader, 1981-.

Morton, Levi P. (1824-1920) Representative from New York, 1879-81. Vice President under Benjamin Harrison, 1889-93. Governor of New York, 1895-97.

Morton, Oliver (1823-77) Governor of Indiana, 1861-67. Senator from Indiana, 1867-77.

Morton, Rogers C.B. (1914-) Representative from Maryland, 1963-71. Chairman of the Republican National Committee, 1969-71. Secretary of the Interior, 1971-75. Secretary of Commerce, 1975-76.

Nixon, Patricia Ryan (1912-) First Lady of the United States, 1969-74.

Packwood, Robert (1932-) Senator from Oregon, 1969-.

Payne, Sereno E. (1843-1914) Representative from New York, 1883-87, 1889-1914.

Pettis, Shirley (1924-) Representative from California, 1975-79.

Platt, Thomas C. (1833-1910) Representative from New York, 1873-77. Senator, 1881-1909.

Rankin, Jeannette (1880-1973) Suffragette and representative from Montana, 1917-19, 1941-43.

Reagan, Nancy (1923-) First Lady of the United States, 1981-.

Reid, Charlotte Thompson (1913-) Representative from Illinois, 1963-71. Member of House Appropriations Committee.

Rhodes, John (1916-) Representative from Arizona, 1953-83.

Rogers, Edith Nourse (1881-1960) Representative from Massachusetts, 1925-60. Member of House Civil Service, Foreign Affairs, and Veterans Affairs Committees.

Rumsfeld, Donald (1932-) Representative from Illinois, 1963-69. Secretary of Defense, 1975-77.

St. George, Katharine Price Collier (1896-1983) Representative from New York, 1947-65. Member of House Rules Committee.

Scott, Hugh (1900-) Representative from Pennsylvania, 1941-45, 1947-59. Senator, 1959-77. Chairman of the Republican National Committee, 1948-49.

Simpson, Alan K. (1931-) Senator from Wyoming, 1979-.

Smith, Margaret Chase (1897-) Representative from Maine, 1940-49. Senator, 1949-73.

Smith, Mary Louise (1914-) Chairman of the Republican National Committee, 1974-77.

Smith, Virginia Dodd (1911-) Representative from Nebraska, 1975-. Member of House Appropriations Committee.

Snowe, Olympia J. (1947-) Representative from Maine, 1979-. Member of House Foreign Affairs Committee.

Stevens, Ted (1923-) Senator from Alaska, 1968-.

Thompson, Ruth (1887-1970) Representative from Michigan, 1951-57. Member of House Judiciary Committee.

Thurmond, Strom (1902-) Governor of South Carolina, 1947-51. Senator from South Carolina, 1954-56, 1956-. President pro tempore, 1981-87.

Tower, John G. (1925-) Senator from Texas, 1961-85. Served in the Navy during World War II.

Trumbull, Lyman (1813-96) Justice of the Supreme Court of Illinois, 1848-53. Senator from Illinois, 1855-73.

Vander Jagt, Guy (1931-) Representative from Michigan, 1966-.

Weed, Thurlow (1797-1882) Journalist and politician. Editor of Albany *Evening Journal*, 1830-62. Associate of Seward and Greeley. Vigorous supporter of Lincoln.

Weis, Jessica McCullough (1901-1963) Representative from New York, 1959-63.

Wilmot, David (1814-68) Representative from Pennsylvania, 1845-51. Senator, 1861-63. Authored the famous Wilmot Proviso in 1848 prohibiting slavery in the territories.

Wilson, Pete (1933-) Senator from California, 1983-.

Index

Boldface indicates illustrations; *italic* refers to captions.

Adams, John Quincy 60
Adams, Sherman 127
Addams, Jane 46
Agnew, Spiro T. 136, 137, 139, *139*
Agriculture 16, 24, 130
Alaska, purchase of *81*, 84, 152-153
Aldrich, Nelson 91, 103, 105
Allison, William B. 92, 103
American Party 67
Antietam, Battle of 78
Antietam Creek, Md.: Union Army officers 74-75
Antitrust laws *92*, 100, *100*, 105, 106, 159, 160
Arthur, Chester A. 56, **56**, 88, **89**, 90, **90**, 157, 158; Civil Service reforms 88, 90, *90*
Atomic energy 26, 29, 157

Baker, Howard H., Jr. 148, 160
Banks, Nathaniel P. 64, 160
Bates, Edward 71, 76, **77**
Blaine, James G. 45, 71, 90, 91, **91**, 92, 158
Bolton, Frances P. 54, **54**
Bovay, Alvan 60, 63
Breckinridge, John 72, 73
Bricker, John W. 122
Brooke, Edward W. **50-51**, 51
Brooks, Preston 65, **66**, 154
Brown, John: raid on Harpers Ferry 71
Bryan, William Jennings 94, 97, 104
Buchanan, James 66, 67, 68, 69, 74
Bull Moose Party *see* Progressive Party
Burger, Warren **139**
Bush, George 142, 160
Butler, Andrew P. 65, **66**
Butler, Benjamin 76, 91
Butler, Nicholas Murray 42, 46, **46-47**, 158

Cameron, Simon P. 71, 76, 150
Campaigning, political 49, 127; Republican campaign memorabilia cover, **7, 59, 89, 92, 119, 120, 122, 133**
Cannon, Joseph G. **102**, 103, 105
Carswell, G. Harrold 137
Carter, Jimmy 140, 142, *143*
Cartoons, political **66, 87, 95, 100, 104,** 105, **107**

Chase, Salmon P. 14, 61, 63-64, 71, 76, **77**, 150, 152, 160
Chou En-lai **137,** 138
Civil rights: Civil Rights Acts 82, *129*, 134, 152, 157; school desegregation 130, *131,* 157; *see also* Slavery
Civil Service Commission 90, *90*
Civil War 10, 13, 14, *62,* 73-78, *83,* 152, 153, 154; Union Army officers **74-75**
Clay, Henry 45, 60, 61
Clay, Lucius 36, 38
Cleveland, Grover 90, 91, *91,* 92, 93, 94
Colfax, Schuyler 64
Colleges, land-grant 24, 69, 84, 91, 146, 155
Connally, John 142
Conservation 18, 20, 100, 106, 151, 154
Constitution, U.S. 60, 146, 147; 13th Amendment 10, 78, 160; 14th Amendment 82, 133, 156; 15th Amendment 82, 154; 16th and 17th Amendments 106; 19th Amendment 152; 25th Amendment 139, *139,* 140
Coolidge, Calvin 38, **39, 57,** 110, 111, 112, 115-116; laissez-faire creed 111, 116, *133,* 134; quoted 38, 58, *113,* 115-116, 156; with Sioux headdress **113;** *see also* Day-by-day calendar
Cummins, Albert B. 99, 161

Davis, Jefferson 74, 150, 153
Dawes, Charles G. 42, 157, 158, 161
Day-by-day calendar (listing of Republican-related accomplishments) 150-160
Debates, political: Lincoln-Douglas 69, **70,** 71; Nixon-Kennedy 132, 158; Reagan-Carter-Anderson 142
Depression, economic 93, 94; *see also* Great Depression
Dewey, George **96,** 98
Dewey, Thomas E. 121, 122, *122,* 123, 126, 152; 1948 campaign button **122**
Dole, Elizabeth Hanford 141
Dole, Robert J. 140, 161
Dondero, George **34,** 35
Douglas, Stephen A. 63, 68, 69, **70,** 71, 72, 73, 76
Dred Scott case 67-68, *68,* 69, 152

Dulles, John Foster 127, 128, 154, 158
DuPont, Francis S. 36
Dwyer, Florence P. 54, **55**

Edison, Thomas Alva **111**
Education 24, 131, 132, 146, 159
Ehrlichman, John 137, 138
Eisenhower, Dwight D. **9, 28, 57,** 124, 125-128, **126, 129,** 130, 132; civil rights actions 130, *151,* 157; interstate highway modernization 36, 128, 155; peace programs 29, 128, 130; quoted 8, 29, 58, *124,* 127; *see also* Day-by-day calendar
Eisenhower, Mamie **126**
Emancipation Proclamation 78, 150, 157, 160; reading of first draft **77;** signing 10, **10-11**

Fall, Albert B. *111,* 112, 152
Faubus, Orval E. 130, *131*
Fish, Hamilton 84
Flanders, Ralph 127
Food for Peace Program 128, 130
Ford, Gerald R. **58, 139,** 139, 140, 147; quoted 58, *139*
Ford, Henry **111**
Forest preservation 18, 20, 155
Free enterprise system 38
Free Soil Party 16, 61, 64, 152
Frémont, John C. 66, 67, 155

Garfield, James A. 56, **56,** 88, **89;** assassination 88, *88*
Gettysburg Address 13, 152, 159
Giddings, Joshua 63, 64
The Gilded Age 86-93
Gilder, George 143
Goethals, George W. 33
Goldwater, Barry 132, 134, 136; 1964 presidential campaign 138, 142, 145, "Gold Water" can **133;** quoted 145-146
Goodell, Charles 137
Gorgas, William C. 33, 151
Grand Old Party (Republican label) 94, 95
Grant, Ulysses S. 30, 56, **56,** 80, 83, **83,** 84, 86, *111,* 152, 153, 154, 158
Great Depression 53, 116, *117,* 118, 120; crash of Wall Street *114,* 116; Hoovervilles 117; soup kitchen **117**
Greeley, Horace 60, 64, 76, 86, 156
Grimes, John 83
Grow, Galusha 64

Haldeman, H.R. 137, 138
Half-Breeds (Republican faction) 86, 88, 90
Halleck, Charles W. 121, 123
Hamlin, Hannibal **73,** 154, 158, 161
Hanna, Marcus Alonzo 92, 94,**94**
Harding, Warren G. **57,** 58, 111, **111,** 112, 155, 156, 158, 159, 160
Harrison, Benjamin 20, 56, **56,** 92-93, *92,* 154, 156
Hatfield, Mark 136
Hay, John **32,** 33, 97, 150
Hayes, Rutherford B. 56, **56,** 86, 88, **88,** 150, 151, 152, 155
Haynesworth, Clement 137
Heckler, Margaret 54, **55,** 161
Helper, Hinton 70, 71
Herter, Christian A. 130
Hickel, Walter 137
Hiss, Alger 125, 159
Hobart, Garret A. 97
Homestead Act 16, *79,* 84, 154; homesteaders **78-79**
Hoover, Herbert **52-53,** 53, **57,** 112, **114,** 116-118; quoted 58; 112; *see also* Day-by-day calendar
Hoover, J. Edgar 136
Hughes, Charles Evans **40,** 41, 109, **109,** 110, 112, 150, 159

Interstate Highway System 30, 36, **36-37,** 128, *129,* 147, 155
Iran-contra affair 144, 148
Iran hostage crisis 142

Jackson, Andrew 60
Jackson, Mich.: Republican meeting place 8, 64, 155
Javits, Jacob 133
Jefferson, Thomas 60
Johnson, Andrew 14, 56, **56,** 80-81, 82; impeachment 82-83, 151, 152
Johnson, Hiram 99, 110, 111, 119
Johnson, Lyndon B. 132, *133,* 134, 136, 150

Kansas-Nebraska Act 63, 64, 152
Keifer, J. Warren 91
Kellogg, Frank B. 42, 159, 161
Kellogg-Briand Treaty 150, 156, 157, 160
Kemp, Jack 143
Kennedy, John F. 132, 133, *133,* 134, 157, 158
Kirkpatrick, Jeanne **141**
Kissinger, Henry 42, 137, *137,*

138, 140
Know-Nothing Party 65, 67
Knox, Frank *119*
Korean War 124, 125, 127

Labor 41; child labor 99, 154; National Eight Hour Law **82;** women's rights *83*
LaFollette, Robert 99, 106, 110, 111, 115
LaFollette, Robert, Jr. 119
Land-Grant Act *see* Morrill Act
Landon, Alfred M. 119, *119,* 145; 1936 campaign button *119*
Law and order 51
Leach, Jim 144
Lee, Robert E. 80, 153
Liberty Party 61, 64
Lincoln, Abraham **57,** 61, **62,** 64, 67, 69, **70,** 71-74, **75,** 76-80; assassination 80, 153; 1860 presidential campaign 49, 71-73, *72, 87,* poster **73;** Emancipation Proclamation 10, **10-11,** 77, 78, 150, 157, 160; Gettysburg Address **12-13,** 13, 152, 159; quoted 10, 13, 14, 41, 56, 69, *70, 72,* 74, 146, 151, 157; second inaugural 14, **14-15,** 80; *see also* Day-by-day calendar
Lindsay, John V. 136
Little Rock, Ark.: school desegregation 130, **131,** 157
Lockwood, Belva Ann Bennett 86, *88*
Lodge, Henry Cabot 94, 109, 110

MacArthur, Douglas 123, 125
McCarthy, Joseph R. 125, 126, 127, 132
McClellan, George B. **75,** 80
MacDonald, Thomas 36
McKinley, William 38, 56, **57,** 91, 94, **95,** 97, *98,* 150; assassination 97, 157
MacNary, Charles L. 121
Madison, James 60, 146
Manila Bay, battle of **96**
Martin, Joseph W., Jr. 123, 150, 162
May, Catherine 54, **54**
Miller, William 134
Mission 66 (National Park Service program) 22
Mitchell, John 136, 138
Morella, Constance **141**
Morrill, Justin S. 24, **25,** 84, 91, 133
Morrill Act 24, 84, 155

Nast, Thomas, cartoon by **87**

National Eight Hour Law: lithograph **82**
Nixon, Richard M. **58,** 127, **129,** 130, 132-134, **135,** 136-140, 159; quoted 58; resignation *135,* 140; visit to China **137,** 138
Nobel Peace Prize 42, **43;** winners 42, 46, 103, 154, 157, 159, 161
Normandy invasion: Eisenhower with troops **124-125**
Norris, George W. 99, 119
Nuclear weapons 124, 130, 131, 133

O'Connor, Sandra Day **141**
Olympic (battleship) **96**

Panama Canal, construction of **32-33,** 33, 90, *91,* 100, **101;** cartoon **95**
Pan-American Union 45, 158
Parks, national 22, *99,* 155
Pendleton Act 88, 90, *90,* 150, 152
Pennington, William 69
Penrose, Boies 92
Percy, Charles 136
Phillips, Kevin 137
Pinchot, Gifford 20, **20-21,** 106, 154
Platt, Orville 92
Progressive Party *107,* 108, 109
Promontory, Utah: completion of transcontinental railroad 30, **30-31, 84-85,** 154

Quay, Matt 92

Radical Republicans (faction) 76, 80, 82, 83, 84, 133
Railroad, first transcontinental 8, 30, 63, 67, 69, 84; completion 30, **30-31, 84-85,** 154
Rankin, Jeannette 54, 152, 162
Reagan, Ronald 58, **58,** 136, 140, 142, 143, **143,** 144, 148
Reconstruction era 78-86
Reed, Thomas B. 91, 94, 95
Reid, Charlotte T. 54, **55**
Republican Party: creation of 8, 60, 63, 64, 65, 152; day-by-day calendar of accomplishments 150-160; elephant as symbol 73, *87,* **87;** members of note 160-162; Presidents 56, **56-57,** 58, *see also* individual names; women leaders 6, 54, **54-55, 141**
Ripon, Wisc.: origin of Republican Party 8, 63, 65, 152;

schoolhouse **9,** 65
Ripon Society *133,* 134, 144
Rockefeller, Nelson 132, 133, 140
Romney, George 134, 136
Roosevelt, Franklin D. 112, 118,
  119, *119,* 120, *120,* 121, 122,
  122
Roosevelt, Theodore **18-19, 43,
  57,** 94, 97, **98,** 99, **99,** 100, **101,**
  102-111; conservation pro-
  grams 18, 20, 100; Nobel Peace
  Prize winner 42, *104,* 157; political cartoons **100, 104, 107;**
  quoted 18, 56, *100; see also*
  Day-by-day calendar
Root, Elihu 42, 106, 108, 159
"Rough Riders" (First U.S. Volunteer Cavalry) **98,** 99, 108,
  153-154, 155
Ross, Edmund 83
Russo-Japanese War 42, **42-43,**
  103, 155, 156; peace treaty 42,
  103, **104,** 154, 157

St. Lawrence Seaway **34-35,** 35,
  154, 156
Schurz, Carl 86
Scott, Dred 67, **68,** 68
Scott, Hugh 133
Scranton, William 134, 147
Seaton, Frederick 22, **22-23**
Seward, William H. 61, 63, 64,
  67, 71, 76, **77, 81,** 84, 151, 152,
  160
Sherman, James S. 158
Sherman, John 64, 91, 92
Sherman, William T. 91, 152,
  153, 159
Sherman Antitrust Act *92, 100,*
  159, 160
Sioux Indians 113
Slavery: abolition of 8, 10, 60,
  61, 63, 76, 77, 78, 155; opposi-
  tion to, as Republican heritage
  64, 65, 66-67, 147; *see also*
  Emancipation Proclamation
Smith, Margaret Chase 54, **55,**
  150, 155, 157, 162
Soup kitchen, Depression-era
  117
Spanish-American War *94,* 95,
  96, 99, 156, 157, 159; battle of
  Manila Bay **96;** charge up San
  Juan Hill *98,* 153-154, 155
Stalwarts (Republican faction) 88
Stanford, Leland 30, **31,** 154
Stanton, Edwin **77,** 82, 83, 150,
  156
Stassen, Harold 123, 130
Stephens, Alexander 81

Stevens, Thaddeus 76, 79
Stevenson, Adlai 127, 130, 132
Stockman, David 144
Straus, Oscar S. 102, 160
Strauss, Lewis L. 26, **27**
Sumner, Charles 63, 65, **66,** 76,
  79, 154, 160

Taft, Robert A. 121, 123, 126,
  127, 156
Taft, William H. **44-45,** 45, **48-49,**
  49, **57,** 58, *102,* 104-105, **106,**
  107, 108; *see also* Day-by-day
  calendar
Tammany Hall 86, *87,* 116
Tariff issue 84, 86, *92,* 105, *111;*
  1888 campaign illustration **92**
Teapot Dome affair *111,* 112,
  115, 152
Tennessee Valley Authority
  (TVA) 99, 128, 156
Thurmond, Strom 123, 162
Tree of Peace 45, 153
Truman, Harry S. 26, 122, 123,
  125; quoted 60, 117-118

Vandenburg, Arthur H. 121, 123,
  150
Vietnam War 127, 134, 136, 137,

139; Nixon with troops **135**
Voting rights 5, 130, 151, 157

Wade, Benjamin 76
Wade-Davis Bill 80
Warren, Earl 123, 130; 1948 cam-
  paign button **122**
Washburn, Israel 64, 154
Washington, Booker T. 102, 158
Washington, George 74, 149, 159
Watergate scandal 135, 138-139,
  140
Whig Party 61, 63, 65, 67, 152
Wigwam (1860 Republican con-
  vention hall) 72
Willkie, Wendell *120,* 121, 122,
  133; 1940 campaign button **120**
Wilson, James 16, **17**
Wilson, Woodrow *107,* 108, 109,
  109, 110, 112, 152
Women's rights *83, 88,* 151, 152,
  157
Wood, Leonard 111
World War I 103, 108, 109, *109,*
  120, 154; U-boat warfare 108-
  109, *109*
World War II 120, 121, *124,* 125;
  Eisenhower with troops **124-
  125**

Bibliography

The following books are recommended by the author both for
the serious student of American
politics and for the average concerned citizen.

Boller, Paul F., *Presidential Cam-
paigns,* 1984. Buckley, William F.,
Up From Liberalism, 1959. Bur-
dette, Franklin L., *The Republican
Party: A Short History,* 1968. Bus-
bey, L. White, *Uncle Joe Cannon:
The Story of a Pioneer American,*
1927. Crane, Philip M., *The Sum
of Good Government,* 1976. *Goals
for Americans: The Report of the
President's Commission on National
Goals,* 1960. Goldwater, Barry, *The
Conscience of a Conservative,* 1960.
Hays, Brooks, *A Southern Moderate
Speaks,* 1959. Hoover, Herbert, *The
Challenge to Liberty,* 1934. Javits,
Jacob, *Order of Battle: A Republican's Call to Reason,* 1964. Johnson,
Donald B., *The Republican Party
and Wendell Willkie,* 1960. Josephy,
Alvin T., *On the Hill: A History
of the American Congress,* 1979.
Lazarsfeld, Paul; Berelson, Ber-
nard; and Gaudet, Hazel, *The Peo-
ple's Choice: How the Voter Makes
Up His Mind in a Presidential Cam-
paign,* 1944. Leech, Margaret, *In
the Days of McKinley,* 1959. Leo-
pold, Richard W., *Elihu Root and
the Conservative Tradition,* 1954.
Moley, Raymond, *The Republi-
can Opportunity,* 1962. Phillips,
Kevin P., *The Emerging Republican
Majority,* 1969. Republican Com-
mittee on Program and Progress,
Decisions For a Better America, 1960.
Richter, Edward J.; and Bulce,
Berton, *Religion and the Presidency:
A Recurring American Problem,*
1962. Ringer, Robert J., *Restoring
the American Dream,* 1979. Rusher,
William A., *The Making of the New
Majority Party,* 1975. Vandenberg,
Arthur H., Jr., ed., *The Private
Papers of Senator Vandenberg,* 1952.
van der Linden, Frank, *The Real
Reagan,* 1981. Warren, Earl, *The
Memoirs of Earl Warren,* 1977.

AUTHOR'S POSTSCRIPT

From what I've read on political science during my public life and in preparation for this book, I've collected many phrases and quotes. I've been inspired by and gained confidence in Republican literature of the past. Among the most intelligent, forward looking, and worthwhile expressions are the following by Mary Louise Smith of Iowa, a former National Republican Chairman:

". . . America faces such problems as inflation, conservation of resources, and overpopulation, not because we have progressed so little, but because we have accomplished so much in such a relatively short period of time. Unfortunately, solving our problems effectively and—hopefully—conclusively will take time. Doing so demands the total cooperation of the administration, the Congress, and the public alike. . . .

"American institutions have created the most prosperous and educated society in history; these institutions are very often denounced by people who, however intellectual, know the least about them. It is also these people who are the most apathetic toward the one process that best begins to improve society, the political process. New institutions and new approaches are, of course, necessary, not as replacements, but as supplements to our present organizations. . . .

"Realistically, I may not see all of the necessary solutions discovered and implemented in my lifetime. However, optimism is a creative attitude, and I would be in the wrong business if I did not have faith in this country, its people, and the human future in general."

———————

Library of Congress Cataloging-in-Publication Data
Schwengel, Fred, 1906-
   The Republican Party.
   Includes index.
   1. Republican Party (U.S. : 1854-   )—History.
I. Title.
JK2356.S39   1987   324.2734   87-28977
ISBN 0-87491-882-0
ISBN 0-87491-883-9 (pbk.)

Printed in the United States of America by Colortone Press, Creative Graphics Inc., Washington, D.C. 20009

Attention Schools and Corporations: Acropolis books are available at quantity discounts with bulk purchase for educational, business, or sales promotional use. For information, please write to: Special Sales Department, Acropolis Books Ltd., 2400 17th St, NW, Washington, D.C. 20009

REPUBLICAN HERITAGE FOUNDATION

This book is sponsored by the Republican Heritage Foundation, a nonprofit organization dedicated to the study of the economic, social, political, and international problems of this nation. A Republican Heritage Research Fund to underwrite such studies will be created from proceeds of the sale of this publication. All studies sponsored by this fund will be made readily available to the public.

Americans of all political affiliations who are concerned with the vitality of the two-party system can obtain a lifetime membership in the Republican Heritage Foundation by donating $25.00 or more. Send donations to Republican Heritage Foundation, 200 Maryland Avenue, N.E., Suite 301, Washington, D.C. 20002. Members will receive a handsome life membership certificate and periodic reports on the Foundation's activities.

Readers of this book will note that it is not the author's intention to blindly praise the Republican Party nor to criticize the Democratic Party. As a veteran of the legislative arena, the author fully understands that a healthy two-party system serves the public interest. The Democratic Party has its own worthy heritage. It is hoped that this book will promote a better respect between Republicans and Democrats.

ILLUSTRATIONS CREDITS

All illustrations courtesy of the Library of Congress except for the following: pages 8-58, Charles McVicker; cover, pages 7, 59, 119, 120, 122, 144, courtesy of the Smithsonian Institution, Joseph H. Bailey; pages 126, 128-129, National Archives; page 133, Joseph H. Bailey; pages 135, 137, The Nixon Project, National Archives; page 139, courtesy of the Gerald R. Ford Library; page 141, United States Department of Transportation (upper left), Supreme Court Historical Society (upper right), Maryland Eighth Congressional District (lower left), American Enterprise Institute (lower right); page 143, Mary Ann Frankelman-Mink, The White House.

STAFF FOR THIS BOOK

Paul Martin, *Editor*
Cynthia B. Scudder, *Designer*
Helen Virden, Maier Fox, Richard Striner,
   Donald R. Kennon, *Researcher-Writers*
Richard M. Crum, *Picture Caption Writer*
Winthrop D. Scudder, *Illustrations Researcher*
Joseph H. Bailey, *Photographer*
Joanne Hanson, Jean Campbell, Susan E. Malloy,
   Janice Martin, *Staff Assistants*
Dianne L. Hardy, *Indexer*